HEINEMANN SECONDARY HISTORY PROJECT

ELIZABETHAN ENGLAND

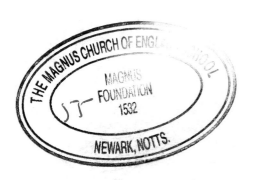

Sue Styles

Heinemann

Heinemann Educational
Halley Court, Jordan Hill, Oxford OX2 8EJ
a division of Reed Educational and Professional
Publishing Ltd

OXFORD MADRID ATHENS FLORENCE
PRAGUE CHICAGO PORTSMOUTH NH (USA) MEXICO
CITY SAO PAULO SINGAPORE KUALA LUMPUR
TOKYO MELBOURNE AUCKLAND IBADAN NAIROBI
KAMPALA GABORONE JOHANNESBURG

Heinemann is a registered trademark of
Reed Educational and Professional Publishing Ltd.

First published 1998

00 99 98
10 9 8 7 6 5 4 3 2 1

British Library cataloguing in Publication data
for this title is available from the British Library.

ISBN 0 345 30858 0

This book is for Alison

Designed and produced by Visual Image
Printed by Mateo Cromo, Spain
Cover design by Wooden Ark
Cover photograph: The Armada Portrait, attributed to George
Gower (1540-96) and painted to celebrate
the defeat of the Armada in 1588. Courtesy of Bridgeman Art
Gallery and Woburn Abbey Bedfordshire.

The authors and publisher would like to thank the following
for permission to reproduce photographs:
Bridgeman Art Gallery: 1.1A, 1.4-4, 2.1E, 3.1B, E, 3.2A, B, 4.3F, 4.5-
1, 5.1A, E, 5.3B, 5.5-1, 6.2A, 7.3D, 7.4-6 British Library: 7.2A
Camera Press: 1.1B, 1.4-1 Corpus Christie College, Cambridge:
7.2B e.t.archive:2.1H, 5.2C, 5.4A, 7.1M, 7.2D Fortean: 1.3B
Fotomas: 2.1C, 2.10, 7.1F,K,L Globe Theatre: 7.2F Hengrave Hall
Centre: 3.3C Hulton Getty: 4.4J Lambeth Palace: 4.2E The
Marquis of Salisbury: 2.1D Methuen: 8.2-6 National Trust: 4.4F,
8.1B National Portrait Gallery: 1.4-2 National Swedish Portraits
Collection: 2.1L Prins Hendrik Maritium Museum: 5.4C Stedelijk
Museum Alkmaar: 5.3A Tiroler Landesmuseum : 5.3I Victoria and
Albert Museum: 1.4-3

The publishers have made every effort to trace copyright holders
of material in this book. Any omissions will be rectified in
subsequent printings if notice is given to the publisher.

The author and publishers gratefully acknowledge the following
publications from which written sources in the book are drawn.
In some sources the wording or sentence structure has been
simplified.

Simon Adams, *England and the World under the Tudors* in *Oxford
Illustrated History of Tudor and Stuart Britain*, (ed. J.Morrill),
OUP, 1996: 8.2-3
A.L. Beier, *The Problem of the Poor in Tudor and Early Stuart
England*, Methuen Lancaster Pamphlets, 1983: 3.3A
J.S. Brewer and W. Bullen (eds.), *Calendar of the Carew MSS. Vol 3*,
1867-70: 6.2D

J. Bruce and T.T. Perowne (eds.), *Correspondence of Matthew Parker*,
NoCLXX, 1853: 4.3C
Lord Burghley, *Memorandum on the Alençon Marriage*, 1579: 5.2B
Calendar of State Papers, Ireland, 1599-1600, 6.2E
William Camden, (ed. Wallace T. MacCaffrey) *The History of the
Most Renowned and Victorious Princess Elizabeth*, University of
Chicago Press, 1970: 1.2B, 4.4D, 5A, 5B, 5.1C, 6.3A, B
William Camden *Annals: The True and Royal History of the famous
Empress Elizabeth, Queen of England*, 1625: 1.5-1
D. Cook, *Documents and Debates*, Macmillan, 1980: 2.1-I, J, 4.3A
G.R. Elton, E*ngland under the Tudors*, Methuen, 1963: 3.5-2, 6.3C,
8.1C
W.H. Frere and C.E. Douglas (eds.), *Puritan Manifestos*, 1907: 4.3E
Henry Gee, *The Elizabethan Prayer Book*, London 1902: 1.1C
M.A.E. Green (ed.), *State Papers Domestic, Addenda Vol. XXI*,
London, 1869: 6.1B
J.R.R. Green, *A Short History of the English People*, Macmillan,
1874,(1911): 1.5-4, 3.5-3
J. Guy, in *Oxford Illustrated History of Tudor and Stuart Britain* (ed. J
Morrill) OUP, 1996: 2.1F
John Guy, *Tudor England*, OUP, 1988: 8.2-5
C. Haigh (ed.), *The Reign of Elizabeth I*, Macmillan, 1984: 1.1D, E,
1.5-1-5
C. Haigh, in *Oxford Illustrated History of Tudor and Stuart Britain*
(ed. J. Morrill), OUP, 1996: 2.1A, 6.2F
William Harrison, *The Description of England*, 1587: 3.1A
Victor von Klarvill, in *Queen Elizabeth I and some Foreigners*, The
Bodley Head, 1928: 4.4A
E. Lodge, *Illustrations of British History in the Reign of Elizabeth*, Vol.
2, 1838: 5.2A
N. Egbert McClure, P. Williams (eds.), *The Letters and Epigrams of
Sir John Harington*, Philadelphia, 1930: 1.5-3
Z. Nuttall, (ed.), *New Light on Drake: A Collection of Documents
relating to his Voyage of Circumnavigation, 1577-80*, Vol. 34,
Hakluyt Society, series II, 1914: 5.3C
D.M. Palliser, *quoted from* Sir Thomas Elyot, *Homilies*, in *The Age of
Elizabeth*, Longman, 1983: 3.1C, *The Age of Elizabeth*, 3.5-1
Martin Parker, *The Spanish Armada*, Guild Publishing, 1988: 5.3D
Maria Perry, *The Word of a Prince*, Boydell Press, 1990: 1.2A, 2.1K,
2.2-1, 4.1A, 6.2B, C, D, 8.1A, 8.2-1
G.W. Prothero, *Select Statutes and other Constitutional Documents*,
1913: 4.3D
Geoffrey Regan, *quoted from*, *William Hambarde and Local
Government*, 1594, ed. C. Reed, in *Elizabeth I*, CUP, 1988: 3.1D,
Elizabeth I: 4.2A, 4.3G, 4.4C, 4.4E, 5.2A
M.M. Reece, *The Puritan Impulse 1559-1600*, A.C. Black, 1975: 4.3B
J. Ridley, *The Tudor Age*, Constable, 1988: 7.1M, 7.2C
Conrad Russell, in I*llustrated History of Tudor and Stuart Britain*
(ed. John Murrill), Guild Publishing, London, 1988: 4.1B
A.F. Scott, *Everyone a Witness: The Tudor Age*, White Lion
Publishers, 1975: 7.1A, C-E, G-J, 7.3G
Sir Thomas Smith, *The Governance of England*, 1565: 2.1G, 2.1M, N
P. Stack, *Poverty and Policy in Tudor and Stuart England*, Longman,
1988: 3.3B, 3.4A
Statutes of the Realm, Vol. 4(i), The Act of Supremacy, 4.2B
M.A. Tierney, *Dodd's Church History of England*, Vol. III, 1839-43:
4.4K
Victorian History of the Counties of England, Sussex: 4.4B
Penry Williams, *The Later Tudors*, OUP, 1995: 1.5-2, 5.1B, 5.3E, F, H,
5.4B, 6.1A, 8.2-2, 8.2-4

CONTENTS

CHAPTER 1

QUEEN AND COUNTRY

1.1 Why do people remember Elizabeth I?

Source A

▲ Elizabeth I in the cloth of gold dress and cloak which she wore at her coronation. The painting is probably copied from an original painted in 1559.

Source B

▲ This photograph shows Elizabeth II in the gold dress which she wore at the coronation in 1953.

On 15 January 1559, in Westminster Abbey, Elizabeth Tudor, aged 25, was crowned Queen Elizabeth I of England, France and Ireland, Defender of the Faith.

Nearly 400 years later, on 2 June 1953, also in Westminster Abbey, Elizabeth Windsor, aged 27, was crowned Queen Elizabeth II of the United Kingdom of Great Britain and Northern Ireland and of her other realms and territories, Head of the Commonwealth, Defender of the Faith.

People hailed the start of Queen Elizabeth II's reign as the dawn of a new Elizabethan Age and a new beginning for Britain. Why was this? What was it about the first Queen Elizabeth that made people remember her in the twentieth century, and talk of a 'new Elizabethan Age'?

When Elizabeth Tudor came to the throne in November 1558 after the death of her sister, Queen Mary I, she inherited a country with religious, social and economic problems. England had been involved in a war against France which had cost both money and men. During the war the French captured Calais, which had been the last English-owned part of France. You can read how one of her government officials described England at this time in Source C. Elizabeth's accession to the throne was welcomed by many people who had not been happy during her sister's reign.

Source C

The Queen poor. The realm exhausted. The nobility poor and decayed. Lack of good captains and soldiers. The people out of order. Justice not carried out. All things dear. The French king bestriding the realm, having one foot in Calais and the other in Scotland.

 This was written at the beginning of Elizabeth I's reign by Armigal Waad. He had been a government official under Elizabeth's brother, Edward VI, and also served under Elizabeth I.

Elizabeth's early popularity

Not long after Elizabeth came to the throne people in villages and towns throughout the land started to celebrate 17 November, the day of her accession, as a holiday. By 1576, it had become an official state festival day.

It is quite natural to celebrate a new reign, particularly when things have been hard beforehand. In very different times, people rejoiced at the start of Elizabeth II's reign. The Second World War had ended only eight years before her accession, and Britain, torn and tired by war, looked forward to peace and a new prosperity under the second Elizabeth.

But does Elizabeth I deserve the praise which was heaped upon her by some people during her reign, and the reputation which has followed her down the ages? How far was she the 'Gloriana' and 'Good Queen Bess' of legend? Not everything was wonderful during her reign, and not everyone, as you will find out, would have agreed with the view about Elizabeth expressed in Source D. One interpretation of her reputation is given by a modern historian in Source E. Perhaps you will be able to come to your own conclusions at the end of your study of Elizabeth I.

Source D

These are the great benefits received from God by the happy and long-desired entrance of your Majesty into the imperial throne of this realm, (after the pitiful slaughter and exile of many of your Highness' godly subjects):
The restoration of true religion
The speedy change of wars into peace, and of famine into plenty. All this to your Highness' great honour.

 In 1572 a local official in the town of Warwick wrote about what he felt were the achievements of Elizabeth's reign.

QUESTIONS

1 What similarities can you find between Elizabeth I and Elizabeth II from the information given on these pages?

2 Read Sources C and D. What do they tell you about the problems Elizabeth I found when she came to the throne?

3 Sources D and E both refer to Elizabeth's success as queen. What different reasons do these sources suggest for this success?

Source E

Elizabeth has always seemed the luckiest of the Tudors: she inherited chaos, lived long enough for it to go away, and died before it returned.

The historian Christopher Haigh comments on Elizabeth's apparently successful reign in *The Reign of Elizabeth I*, 1984.

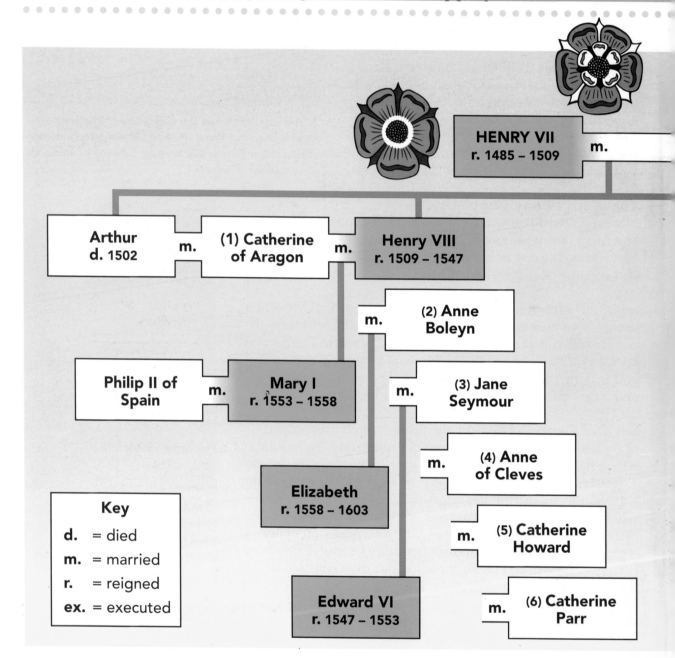

Key

d. = died
m. = married
r. = reigned
ex. = executed

HENRY VII
r. 1485 – 1509   m.

Arthur
d. 1502   m.   (1) Catherine of Aragon   m.   Henry VIII
r. 1509 – 1547

m.   (2) Anne Boleyn

Philip II of Spain   m.   Mary I
r. 1553 – 1558   m.   (3) Jane Seymour

m.   (4) Anne of Cleves

Elizabeth
r. 1558 – 1603   m.   (5) Catherine Howard

Edward VI
r. 1547 – 1553   m.   (6) Catherine Parr

Elizabeth I, born in 1533, was the daughter of Henry VIII and his second wife, Anne Boleyn. In 1485 Elizabeth's grandfather, Henry Tudor, had defeated Richard III at the Battle of Bosworth Field and was declared King Henry VII of England. His younger son, Henry, became King Henry VIII in 1509. Henry VIII's first wife, Catherine of Aragon, gave birth to their daughter, Mary, in 1516. She became Queen Mary I after the death of Henry VIII's only son, Edward VI, in 1553.

The Queen's inheritance

The years between 1485 and 1558 brought rising prosperity to some people and parts of the country, but there were also wars abroad, economic difficulties and religious upheavals (see Sources C and D on page 5).

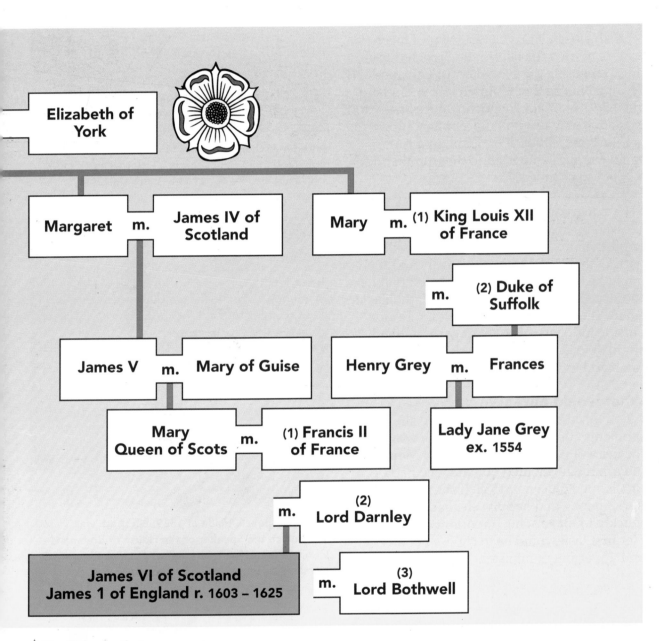

▲ The Tudor family tree.

Religious changes

In the 1530s Henry VIII refused to allow the head of the **Roman Catholic Church**, the **Pope**, to continue to have any power over the Church in England. There were further religious moves towards **Protestantism** during the reign of Edward VI. However, Edward's sister, Mary I, was a devout Roman Catholic and made England officially Catholic again. She married the Catholic king of Spain, Philip II. During her reign she ordered about 300 people to be burnt at the stake for refusing to turn back to Catholicism. Many Protestants fled abroad.

Relations with France and Spain

Henry VIII went to war three times with France and twice with Scotland. The 'auld alliance' between Scotland and France was a constant threat. Both countries saw England as their natural enemy. In 1558 the Catholic Scottish Queen, Mary Stuart (Mary Queen of Scots), married the heir to the French throne, thus cementing the Catholic 'auld alliance'. He became Francis II of France in 1559. England looked to Spain for friendship since Spain, too, was often at war with France. Mary supported her husband, Philip II of Spain, in a war against France which led to the humiliating loss of Calais in 1557.

Mary's marriage to Philip II of Spain had allowed Spain to have some influence over English affairs. England had been friendly with Catholic Spain for many years and there might be trouble if Elizabeth decided that her country should move away from Catholicism again. She certainly would not tolerate any outside influence over her or over England's affairs. Would she marry? If so, whom? You can read her views about marriage in Source B.

What would Elizabeth do?

When Elizabeth came to the throne she faced problems abroad and at home. The words at the head of page 6 are those which Members of Parliament shouted out after she had been proclaimed Queen in 1558. If she really was to reign long and happily she had to work quickly to make some important decisions. Her first task would be to choose her advisers and government ministers to help her to do this.

Elizabeth was only 25 years old when she came to the throne, but she was a highly intelligent and clear-thinking young woman. She spoke a number of languages and was a gifted musician. Elizabeth was, in many ways, wise beyond her years. She had learned a great deal about the problems of power during her youth, especially when she was imprisoned in the Tower of London by Mary I in 1554. So she was used to the intrigues which surrounded life at court.

Source A

She shows such dignity and gentleness as are wonderful at her age. Her mind has no womanly weakness. Her perseverance is equal to that of a man and her memory long keeps what it has picked up. She talks French and Italian as well as she does English, and has often talked to me readily and well in Latin, moderately in Greek. When she writes Greek and Latin nothing is more beautiful than her handwriting.

▲ Roger Ascham, who was Princess Elizabeth's tutor from 1550-1553 wrote this in a letter to his friend John Sturmius, Rector of Strassburg University.

Source B

Concerning marriage, which you so earnestly move me to, I have long since been persuaded, that I was sent into this world by God to think and do those things chiefly which may tend to his glory.
Hereupon I have chosen that kind of life which is most free from the troublesome cares of this world, that I might attend the service of God alone.
Now that the public care of governing the Kingdom is laid upon me, to draw upon me the cares of marriage may seem a point of inconsiderate folly. Yes, to satisfy you, I have already joined myself in marriage to an husband, namely the Kingdom of England.

▲ In this speech, made in 1559, Elizabeth was replying to the Speaker of the House of Commons who had asked her (tactfully) whether she intended to marry and produce an heir to the throne.

QUESTIONS

1 What changes were made to religion in England in the reigns of Henry VIII, Edward VI and Mary I?

2 Why was England friendly with Spain at the start of Elizabeth's reign in 1559?

3 What were the most important problems which Elizabeth had to face at the start of her reign?

Travellers on their way north from London in 1558 would have taken a route which followed the old Roman road, Ermine Street. People in the 16th century knew this as the Great North Road. Until about only 30 years ago a very similar route was taken by the A1 road. This went through many towns and villages which had been there since the 16th century and earlier. Now most of the towns and cities have been by-passed and there is a fast dual-carriageway for most of the journey between London and the north.

On their way north, travellers in 1558 would have had an uncomfortable ride. Roads were bumpy, full of deep holes and rutted by the wheels of carts and wagons. They were dusty and stony in dry weather and muddy and slippery in

▼ **This map shows the main towns and cities in England and Wales in Elizabeth's reign.**

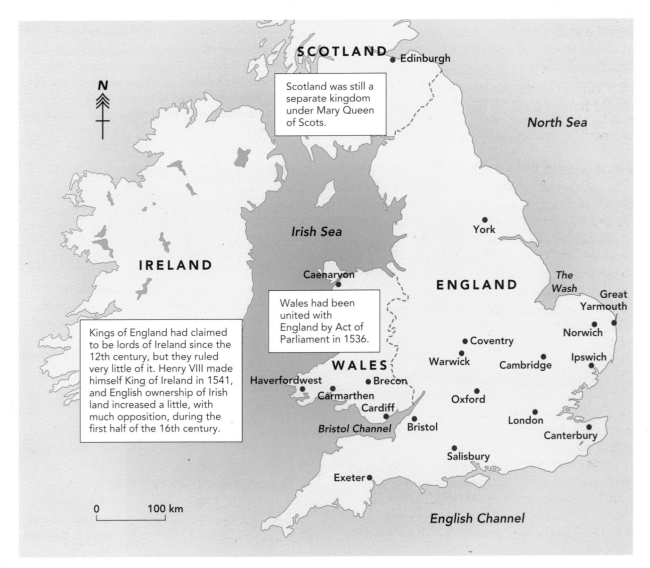

Scotland was still a separate kingdom under Mary Queen of Scots.

Wales had been united with England by Act of Parliament in 1536.

Kings of England had claimed to be lords of Ireland since the 12th century, but they ruled very little of it. Henry VIII made himself King of Ireland in 1541, and English ownership of Irish land increased a little, with much opposition, during the first half of the 16th century.

wet weather. Though it was possible for fast **couriers** to make the journey to Edinburgh in 3 days on horseback, ordinary travellers could be travelling for up to 17 days. They would have passed through small villages in which they might have seen houses like the one shown in Source B. Houses like this were built of stone, timber and sometimes brick. They were lived in by **yeomen**, who were quite well-to-do.

Ordinary villagers lived in houses which sometimes had only one room, and were made of mud or clay reinforced with straw. Travellers might also have seen large country houses like the one shown in Source C. Houses of this size would have been owned by important local families who played a major part in organising local affairs.

The landscape in England and Wales was very varied. On their way north people would have passed by the flat, empty, watery fens of Lincolnshire. They would have

Source A

	c 1520	1990s
London	60,000	6,967,500
Norwich	12,000	126,200
Bristol	10,000	399,600
York	8 000	174,400
Exeter	8 000	107,700
Salisbury	8 000	112,500
Coventry	6 600	303,900
Oxford	5 000	106,700
Great Yarmouth	4 000	89,900
Canterbury	3 000	135,000
Ipswich	3 500	114,000
Cambridge	2 600	100,200
Carmarthen	2 150	57,300
Brecon	1 500	7 500
Haverfordwest	1 500	11,092
Caernarvon	1 000	9 695
Cardiff	1 000	309,400

▲ This table shows the estimated population of the main towns and cities of England and Wales, with their modern equivalents. In 1558 only about 6% of the whole population lived in towns. More people lived in the south than in the north.

Source B

◀ A yeoman's cottage. It was built in the 15th century.

▲ **A large country house in Suffolk, built in 1550.**

travelled through the farming regions of the east midlands where they would see the great open fields which were typical of this and other areas in the midlands and East Anglia before the start of the **enclosure movement** in the late 18th century.

Further north, in Yorkshire and Northumberland, travellers would have looked at a landscape which, in some ways, has changed less than that further south. The Pennine Hills and the Yorkshire Moors were then, as now, wild and wide open to the skies, though it was to be another 200 years or so before the beginning of the industrial developments around Sheffield, Leeds and Newcastle. Travellers in Wales spoke of the moorlands, the mountains and the dense forests which covered much of the country.

One of the biggest differences between Elizabeth I's time and today is the size of the population of England and Wales, and of the cities and the towns. The population, at about 2.8 million in 1558, was small, but it had increased to about 4 million by 1603. The size of the total population in 1558 can, however, never be exactly determined, for the first national **census** was not held until 1801. Any population figures before then are estimates based on available data on, for example, births and deaths. Historians have been able to estimate the size of the main towns and cities in the 16th century: you can see these in Source A.

SUMMARY

In 1558 in England and Wales:

► there was a small, but rising population
► the countryside was very varied
► more people lived in the country than in the towns
► more people lived in the south than in the north
► houses were sometimes made from local stone or brick, but more often from timber, mud and clay
► roads were unsurfaced and travel was generally slow

Many portraits of Elizabeth were painted during her reign, by both English and foreign artists. Elizabeth was very concerned about how she was portrayed. She hated paintings to show her as she really was, particularly as she grew older. She wanted her portraits to show her as a powerful, commanding figure, with none of the wrinkles and weaknesses which age can bring even to a queen.

Source 1

▲ This painting, by an artist whose name we do not know, shows Elizabeth as a princess, aged 13. It was probably painted at the request of her father, Henry VIII.

Source 2

▲ This portrait of Elizabeth, possibly painted by the Spaniard Zuccaro in about 1575, was used as a model for many later portraits of the Queen.

Source 3

▲ Isaac Oliver, an English artist, painted this miniature of Elizabeth in the late 1590s.

Source 4

▲ This was painted by Marcus Gheeraerts the Younger, who came from the Netherlands, in about 1592.

1 Look at the portraits of Elizabeth shown in Sources 1-4 on this page. Look also at the 'Armada Portrait' on the front cover of this book. This was painted in about 1588, probably by the Englishman George Gower.

  a Write a short description of how Elizabeth appears to you in each portrait.

  b Look at the descriptions you have written in your answer to question 1a. Do you think Elizabeth would have liked your descriptions of her? Explain your answer.

2 Can you see any similarities or differences between the portraits? What changes do they show between the earliest and the latest to be painted?

3 Are any of the portraits making a more specific point than others? If so, what is this?

4 Now try to suggest and explain the various purposes which royal portraits were supposed to have at this time.

1.5 Exercise: the Royal Image — Writings

Source 1

Nothing shall ever bury the glory of her name, for her happy and renowned memory still liveth and shall for ever live in the minds of men as of one who, in wisdom and successful government, surpassed all the princes since the days of the Roman Emperor Augustus.

▲ William Camden, who lived from 1551 – 1623, wrote this at the end of his book on the history of Elizabeth's reign.

Source 2

She seems to me incomparably more feared than her sister and gives her orders and has her way as absolutely as her father did.

▲ Count Feria, the Spanish Ambassador, made this comment after one of his early meetings with Elizabeth after she became Queen.

Source 3

When she smiled, it was pure sunshine, that everyone did choose to bask in, if they could; but then came a storm from a sudden gathering of clouds, and the thunder fell in wondrous manner on all alike.

▲ This was written by Sir John Harington, Elizabeth's god-son.

Source 4

No nobler group of ministers ever gathered round a council-board than those who gathered round the council-boards of Elizabeth. But she was the instrument of none. She listened, she weighed, she used or put by the counsels of each in turn, but her policy as a whole was her own. It was a policy, not of genius, but of good sense.

▲ The 19th century historian, JRR Green, gave this view of Elizabeth in a book published in 1874.

Source 5

The myth of Gloriana was severely dented by the end of her reign. To some Spanish rule (or even Scottish) seemed preferable. There was a widespread wish in her last years that the old woman would be gone: the French ambassador recorded in 1597 that Elizabeth's government 'was little pleasing to the great men and the nobles, and if by chance she should die it is certain that the English would never again submit to the rule of a woman'.

▲ Christopher Haigh, a modern historian, in *The Reign of Elizabeth I*, 1984.

1 Read Sources 1-5. These Sources contain a number of different judgements about Elizabeth I. Find as many of these as you can and list them in a table like this:

2 a Now use the information which you have put in the table to write a few paragraphs describing the various judgements which people have made about Elizabeth I.

b Why do you think they differ?

For Elizabeth			Critical of Elizabeth		
Author	Date	Judgement	Author	Date	Judgement

CHAPTER 2

QUEEN AND GOVERNMENT

2.1 How was Elizabethan England governed?

England in the 16th century was ruled quite differently from the way in which it is governed today, although there are some similarities with present-day government. We still have a monarch. We have a Parliament, and ministers who have the responsibility for carrying out Parliament's decisions. There are, however, more differences than similarities. In the 16th century, the monarch really did rule the country. Kings and queens made decisions about all aspects of government, in peace or war, and made sure that these decisions were carried out. They were helped in this by a Royal Council, where important men – bishops, nobles and knights – were invited to give advice to the monarch. But the Council's advice was not necessarily accepted. The positions of power these men held were entirely dependent upon the Queen's support. The government, quite simply, was the Queen.

Elizabeth was also helped by a number of officers of state who were part of the Royal Court, and by a Parliament. In Elizabeth's time there were no rules, as there are today, as to when the next Parliament should meet or how long it should last – the Queen decided. Members of Parliament were elected to the **House of Commons**, but very few people in the country and only men, had the right to vote in elections.

Monarchs today still give what is called the '**Royal Assent**' to bills before they become Acts of Parliament. Unlike Elizabeth I, however, 20th century monarchs play no real part in deciding what government policy should be, neither (unlike Elizabeth I) would they refuse to give the Royal Assent to bills.

The Royal Court

Since the Queen was at the centre of the government of the country, all the members of the Royal Court who surrounded and served her were drawn into this centre of power.
It was huge, numbering over 1,000 men and women. Many people carried out a wide range of duties. There were people who did domestic jobs like the Queen's pages and maids. There were those whose responsibility it was to feed and look

Source A

Rulership required that the sovereign be an active political manager, commanding the energies and taming the rivalries of politicians within the Court circle. On the national stage, in order to win the confidence of the politically important people, she cultivated her popularity as eagerly as any modern elected head of government.

▲ Christopher Haigh, *The Reign of Elizabeth I*, 1984.

Source B

There were 200 young gentlemen, clad in white velvet and 300 in black velvet and 1500 more on horseback ready to receive the Queen. The banquet did so exceed that at other places. A show representing the fairies was seen and a rich jewel was presented to the Queen.

▲ This is from an eyewitness account of Elizabeth's visit to Hengrave Hall in Suffolk in August 1578. After her visit Elizabeth knighted the owner, Sir Thomas Kytson.

after the vast number of people who were part of the court or visitors to it. There were chaplains and physicians and the Dean of the Chapel Royal (a post which still exists today). There were people who looked after the horses and the royal palaces. The Royal Court was mainly based at the Palace of Whitehall.

Royal Progresses

From time to time, the Queen visited and stayed at the homes of the nobility and other important people. On these visits, known as the 'royal progresses', all those who looked after the Royal Court went with the Queen. People who entertained the Queen on her progresses spent vast sums of money in the hope of impressing her (see Source B page 15). She might, for example, reward them with an important post which would bring them financial reward or greater social standing, or both. A few people became very rich as a result of royal rewards for service to the Queen. William Cecil (made Lord Burghley in 1571), who served Elizabeth loyally until his death in 1598, was able to found a **dynasty** which has lasted until today. Sir Walter Raleigh also became very rich as a result of the Queen's favours.

Patronage

Anyone who wanted to be noticed by the Queen, to be given an important job or to have their plays, poetry or music approved, would attend the Royal Court. Each year the Queen received thousands of requests from people seeking favours from herself and from her court, many of whom were patrons (gave financial and social support) to artists, writers, musicians, architects and craftsmen. Patrons were often praised and glorified in a portrait, in words or in music (see Source C). One of the greatest patrons of Elizabeth's reign was Robert Dudley, Earl of Leicester (see Source E). He supported, amongst others, Philip Sidney and Edmund Spenser, both of whom became famous poets.

The Privy Council

During the reigns of Henry VII and Henry VIII, the large Royal Council had become less

Source C

▲ This picture shows the poet, George Gascoigne, presenting a manuscript of his poems to the Queen in 1576. The picture was included in the manuscript, showing how important the queen's patronage was.

Source D

▲ William Cecil, Lord Burghley, drawn during Elizabeth's reign by an unknown artist.

involved in helping the monarch to make important decisions. On her accession Elizabeth I chose as her chief advisers a small group of 12 men from the 58 who formed the Royal Council. This group was known as the Privy Council. Its reponsibilities were to assist the queen in making decisions about home and foreign policy, to ensure that all political decisions were carried out and to keep the government in touch with the rest of the nation through the people who held power in the counties and the towns (see this chapter, pages 22-3). The Privy Council kept close links with special councils, made up of important local men, in the North and in Wales. They tried to ensure that these areas were well informed about royal policies and that good order was kept there.

The number of people who belonged to Elizabeth's Privy Council varied throughout her reign from 12 to 20. Elizabeth tried to choose advisers with a range of views. There were, as a result, some issues over which her Privy Councillors disagreed with both the Queen and with each other, for example whether or not to go to war with Spain (see Chapters 4 and 5).

Elizabeth's Councillors

William Cecil, later Lord Burghley, was one of Elizabeth's most important councillors, and her first Principal Secretary. He was her Lord Treasurer from 1572 until his death in 1598. In this post he had to look after the Queen's finances, with which she had to run her court as well as the country.

Another important member was Robert Dudley, Earl of Leicester, a man as impulsive and rash as Burghley was cautious and careful. He often disagreed with Cecil, and resented his influence over the Queen. Leicester was a great favourite of Elizabeth and at one time it was thought that she might marry him. She did not marry him, or any other man, as you will see.

Sir Francis Walsingham had a great deal to do with foreign affairs between 1568-1590. He effectively organised a large secret service which helped to find out about plots against Elizabeth.

Source E

▲ The Earl of Leicester was painted by Steven van der Mewen, a Dutchman, early in Elizabeth's reign.

Source F

Elizabeth I carefully managed her own policy. She knew her own mind; her instinct to power was without mistake. When her Privy Councillors tried to manipulate her, they were rarely successful; she would lose her temper and the matter would rest.

Yet she repeatedly postponed important decisions: unless panicked she could put things off for years. Her successive ditherings drove Sir William Cecil (later Lord Burghley), her chief courtier and Privy Councillor, to distraction.

She wavered over the trial and execution of Mary Queen of Scots in 1585-7; and would not decide whether or not to offer help to the Dutch Protestants against Philip II.

▲ The historian John Guy, writing in 1988, explains some of the strengths and weaknesses of Elizabeth I as Queen.

Parliament

Elizabeth was entitled, as queen, to issue **proclamations** about anything which she wished to be done. However, if she wanted to be certain that something happened, she could give it the force of law, by having an Act of Parliament passed. The only other reason the Queen would have to call Parliament was when she needed money. Parliament's consent was necessary for the collection of taxes from the country. Parliament discussed whatever the monarch wished to lay before it and decisions which the monarch needed to become law. The Queen could dismiss a Parliament whenever she wanted.

Throughout the middle ages the **House of Lords** was far more important than the House of Commons. By Elizabeth's reign this was changing. Though the members of the House of Lords were more powerful than those in the Commons there were fewer of them – under 100 in the Lords as compared with nearly 400 in the Commons. This was partly because the **dissolution of the monasteries** by Henry VIII in the late 1530s removed the abbots of the larger monasteries from the Lords. It was also because more towns were becoming **boroughs** and so were entitled to have a Member of Parliament. This made the House of Commons larger.

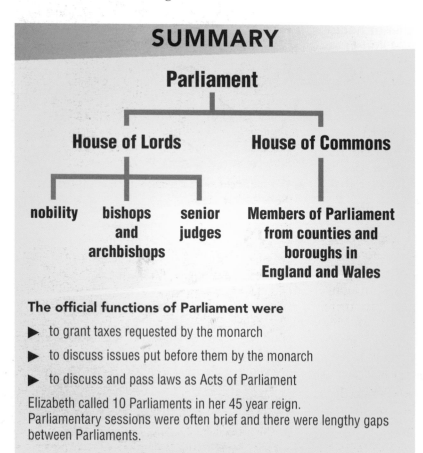

SUMMARY

Parliament

House of Lords — nobility; bishops and archbishops; senior judges

House of Commons — Members of Parliament from counties and boroughs in England and Wales

The official functions of Parliament were

▶ to grant taxes requested by the monarch

▶ to discuss issues put before them by the monarch

▶ to discuss and pass laws as Acts of Parliament

Elizabeth called 10 Parliaments in her 45 year reign. Parliamentary sessions were often brief and there were lengthy gaps between Parliaments.

Source G

The most high and absolute power of the realm of England consists in the Parliament. Every bill or law is read and discussed three times in both houses of Parliament. Therefore no man can complain but must accept it and obey it. That which is done by this consent is taken for law. And the consent of Parliament is taken to be every man's consent.

▲ Adapted from *The Governance of England* written in 1565 by Sir Thomas Smith. He was at one time Elizabeth I's ambassador in France.

During the first half of the 16th century Parliament played an increasingly important role in carrying out the monarch's wishes by making them law. Elizabeth's father, Henry VIII, had, for example, used Parliament during the 1530s to legalise his break with the Pope and the dissolution of the monasteries. His son, Edward VI and his daughter, Mary I, had also used Acts of Parliament to alter religious practice in England. As a result, Parliament, especially the House of Commons, began to feel that it should have more influence over important decisions made for the country and not just be there at the beck and call of the monarch.

Elizabeth and her Parliaments did not always agree over important issues. Two of the most important were freedom of speech (whether Parliament should be allowed to discuss whatever it wanted) and the succession – the problem of whether (and whom) Elizabeth would marry so that she would have an heir.

Freedom of speech

Henry VIII had first granted the House of Commons freedom to discuss matters of policy introduced into the House in 1523. But what did 'freedom of speech' mean? To some, including the Elizabethan MP Peter Wentworth, it meant that the Commons should be able to discuss whatsoever it wished without worrying about the Queen's disapproval and being told to 'take heed what you do, the Queen's Majesty liketh not

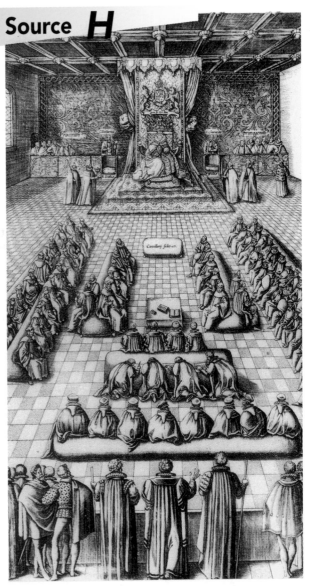

Source H

▲ This woodcut shows Elizabeth on her throne in the House of Lords.

QUESTIONS

1 Describe

   a some of the similarities and
   b some of the differences between the monarch's role in government in the 16th century and the monarch's role today.

2 Explain how the system of 'patronage' worked. Why was this important both to those who gave and to those who received patronage?

3 Use the text and the sources on pages 15-18 (and look back to chapter 1) to write an account of

   a Elizabeth I's strengths as Queen.
   b her weaknesses as Queen

4 Explain the work of

   a the Privy Council and
   b Parliament.

5 Read Source G. Explain why Sir Thomas Smith thinks that Parliament is important.

of such a matter.' The Queen's definition of freedom of speech was rather more restricted (Source I). Members of the House of Commons protested about this on many occasions, but in the end they had to accept the limitations placed on them.

Had Members of the House of Commons respected the Queen less there might have been much more protest. This is because by the time that Elizabeth came to the throne, Members of Parliament believed that they had the right to be consulted on important matters of state. Elizabeth did not agree with them. She believed that they had no right to discuss religion, the succession or foreign policy unless the Queen invited them to do so. This did not, however, stop them from introducing these issues without Elizabeth's permission.

The problem of the succession

One of the issues which was of great concern to Members of Parliament, especially at the beginning of the reign, was that the Queen should marry and produce an undisputed heir (Source J). You read Elizabeth's thoughts on this early in her reign in Chapter 1 (page 8). Later in the reign, when she was past child-bearing, Parliament pressed her to name her successor so as to avoid uncertainty and possible disputes. She consistently refused to do either of these things (Source K).

One of Parliament's concerns was that Mary Queen of Scots had a claim to the English throne (see the family tree on page 6). At the same time Councillors and MPs did not want a repeat of the situation which arose when Mary I, Elizabeth's sister, married the powerful, Catholic King Philip II of Spain. If Elizabeth married a foreigner, there would have to be no fear of England falling under foreign domination. On the other hand, her marriage to an English noble could lead to rivalry and jealousy with other, equally well-born men. What Parliament did not realise, until Elizabeth brought it forcibly to their attention, was that she would never allow any man, whether he be foreign king or English noble, to be her master.

Elizabeth understood right from the beginning the power which her possible marriage gave her in her dealings with foreign countries. She used her charm and her position to dangle the idea of marriage in front of foreign kings and princes. Erik XIV of Sweden and the French Dukes of Alençon and Anjou were among her disappointed suitors. She used this cleverly to her advantage in pursuing important objectives in foreign policy, especially in relation to France (see Chapter 5). Elizabeth also had her favourites, and enjoyed the company of dashing men like the Earl of Leicester, Sir Walter Raleigh and the Earl of Essex. But she had no intention of being forced into marriage.

Source I

It shall be right that each man of you contain his speech within the bounds of loyalty and good discretion. Her Majesty commands me to tell you it shall be right to say yea or nay to bills with some short declaration of the reason, and in this respect to have a free voice, which is the very true liberty of the House. It is not right, as some suppose, to speak there of all matters such as which form of religion or state of government, shall to their idle brains seem best.

▲ Elizabeth sent this speech to be read as a stern reminder to the House of Commons in February 1593. She is making clear her views about freedom of speech.

Source J

October 26, 1566
The discussion about the succession still goes on. Three days ago the Queen told me that Parliament had offered her votes of £250,000 in taxes on condition that she would agree to marry the man they wanted her to marry. But she refused and said that she would not accept any conditions. She said that the money should be given freely and graciously, as it was for the common good and advantage of the Kingdom.

▲ An extract from the letters of the Spanish Count de Silva, Ambassador to Philip II of Spain.

Source K

Well, the matter whereof they would have made their petition consists in two points: in my marriage and the succession of the crown. I did send them answer by my council, I would marry (although of my own disposition I was not inclined thereunto) but that was not accepted or credited, although spoken by their Queen. I will marry as soon as I can, if God take not the man away whom I want to marry.

▲ Elizabeth tells Parliament in 1566 that they have gone too far in urging her to marry.

Source L

▲ Elizabeth had this portrait of herself painted for Erik XIV of Sweden in 1560. It was sent to Erik to show him that Elizabeth would make an attractive wife.

QUESTIONS

1 a How did Members of Parliament and Elizabeth differ in their understanding of 'freedom of speech'?

b Why was 'freedom of speech' such an important issue to both Elizabeth and Parliament?

2 Why did Parliament keep urging the Queen to marry or name her successor? (Look back also at Chapter I to help you with this.)

3 What do you think were Elizabeth I's reasons behind her refusal to be pushed into marriage by Parliament?

4 Look at Source L. What impression of Elizabeth would Eric get from this portrait?

Local government

The Queen was responsible for ensuring that people throughout the country could live in peace and good order. When travel was as fast as the fastest horse on a muddy or dusty road, when there were no railways and no telephones, it was difficult for central govenment to communicate with those who looked after law and order in the shires of England and Wales.

By 1585 every shire had a **Lord Lieutenant** as the Queen's representative. He was usually a nobleman and often a member of the Privy Council. However, many Lords Lieutenant lived in London and so they relied on **Justices of the Peace** (JPs), who were from well-off but not noble families, to keep the peace in the shires.

JPs had a wide range of responsibilities (see Source M). They dealt with criminal offences in law courts (see page 23). They supervised the work of those who looked after the poor. They also had to make sure that royal proclamations and laws made by Parliament were carried out. There had been JPs since the 12th century, but before Tudor times they had been less important than the Lords Lieutenant. Elizabeth, like the Tudor monarchs before her, made full use of JPs to ensure that peace and order were maintained, and to try to reduce the power of the noble families in the shires. Elizabeth was Queen, and she wanted her rule and **'the Queen's Peace'** to extend over the whole country.

The Law Courts

The Queen also had to make sure that all criminals were suitably punished for their crimes. She also had to see that the trials were as fair as possible and that people, both rich and poor, received a fair hearing. It was virtually impossible to do this in every case, but there was a system of courts which was supposed to deal suitably with different crimes and give people the opportunity to appeal to the queen if they felt that justice had not been done to them.

Justices of the Peace might hear criminal cases themselves, or they could send people for trial in the **Quarter Sessions**, held by the JPs four times a year. These covered wider areas and the JPs from these areas met to try and sentence criminals. Some really serious crimes, for example murder or treason, were sent to be heard at the **Assize Court**. Here

Source M

The Justices of the Peace are men whom the Queen particularly trusts at this time to repress robbers, thieves and vagabonds, also conspiracies, riots and violences. Each of them has authority upon complaint to him of any theft, robbery, manslaughter, murder, violence, riots, unlawful games, or any such disturbance of the peace and quiet of the realm, to commit the persons to the prison.

▲ The duties of Justices of the Peace are described by Sir Thomas Smith in *The Governance of England,*1565.

Source N

For manslaughter, robbery, murder, rape and such crimes as touch not treason, we have by the law of England no other punishment but to hang until they be dead. If a wife kill a husband she shall be burned alive. If the servant kill the master he shall be drawn to the place of execution on a hurdle. Poisoners, if the person die thereof, by a new law made in King Henry VIII's time shall be boiled to death.

For **treason** the pain is more cruel. First to be hanged, taken down alive, his bowels taken out and burned before his face, then to be beheaded, and quartered and the pieces set up in various places.

▲ Sir Thomas Smith, *The Governance of England,*1565. Traitors were people who betrayed their country (committed treason) and they were hung, drawn and quartered as described here.

Source O

▲ This drawing shows a busy session of the royal courts in Westminster Hall, London.

judges from the central law courts in London made what was called a 'circuit' of the main towns of England and Wales twice a year to hear cases and pass sentences.

The law courts which sat in London had developed over many centuries and dealt with a huge variety of cases. For example, one of the functions of the **Court of King's Bench** was to hear appeals from people who felt that they had been treated badly in local courts.

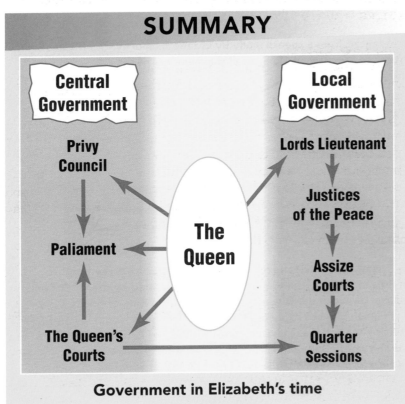

SUMMARY

Central Government

Privy Council

Paliament

The Queen's Courts

The Queen

Local Government

Lords Lieutenant

Justices of the Peace

Assize Courts

Quarter Sessions

Government in Elizabeth's time

The Court of Common Pleas dealt with civil disputes – those between people when no crime had been committed. Both of these courts used what is known as **Common Law**. Cases were dealt with by judges who used the experience of previous, similar cases to decide the outcome.

QUESTIONS

1 Why do you think that Elizabeth wanted to reduce the powers of noble families in the shires (page 22)?

2 What were the main responsibilities of the Justices of the Peace?

3 Punishments in Elizabeth's time (Source N) were very severe. Why was the punishment for treason worse than that for the other crimes mentioned in Source N?

4 What does Source O suggest about the way in which the royal courts of Justice operated in the 16th century?

5 Write a description of government in Elizabeth's time, using the diagram on page 23 and the text and sources on pages 15-24.

2.2 Exercise

Source 1

I want all my decisions to be influenced by good advice. For counsel and advice I shall accept you, my noblemen, and also any such others, who are not noblemen, whom I feel can serve me well.

▲ Adapted from a speech made by Elizabeth, shortly after her accession in 1558, to all the members of the Royal Council.

Source 3

I am your anointed Queen. I will never be by violence forced to do anything. I thank God that I have such qualities that if I were turned out of my realm in my petticoat I would be able to live in any place in Christendom.

▲ Elizabeth I, in an undated speech.

Source 2

How I was deceived! I was expecting a diplomatic mission, but you have brought me a quarrel! I cannot believe that, had your King been here, he would have spoken in such words. As for yourself, you give me the impression of having studied many books, but remaining ignorant of the dealings between Kings.

▲ Part of Elizabeth's speech to the Ambassador from the King of Poland in 1597. The King of Poland was alarmed by the quarrel between the Queen of England and the King of Spain. The Queen had not expected that the Ambassador would criticise her policies, especially since the King of Poland was the son of the Duke of Finland who, almost forty years earlier, had tried to win Elizabeth's hand for Erik XIV of Sweden.

Use Sources 1, 2 and 3, and the text and sources in this chapter to answer these questions.

1 Describe Elizabeth's attitudes towards her position and responsibilities as Queen of England.

2 How did Elizabeth use:

a central government
b local government

to help her to carry out her responsibilities as Queen?

3 In what ways did Elizabeth help noblemen and others to fulfil their ambitions?

CHAPTER 3

PAUPERS, ROGUES AND VAGABONDS

Poor and homeless people increased in number during the 16th century. They had no power to do anything about their situation. They could, however, cause problems merely by not fitting into the general idea of people keeping to their place in society. Everyone was expected to submit to the rules of people in authority over them. Those who had no jobs and no homes were very often neither willing nor able to do this.

As long as people have lived together in societies there have been those who have been less well off than others. This may have been the result of illness, old age or just inability to find a job, but the problem has always been the same: who should look after these people if they could not look after themselves?

It was in the sixteenth century that, for the first time, governments in England tried to create a national system for dealing with the poor and the homeless. Until then individual towns and villages had been left to deal with their own poor people, though there were laws which tried to control and punish wandering beggars. Before Elizabeth's reign

Source A

With us the poor is commonly divided into three sorts.
Some are poor and cannot do anything to help themselves, like the fatherless child, the aged, blind and lame, and the diseased person that is judged to be incurable.
The second sort are poor by accident, as the wounded soldier and the householder who has fallen on bad times.
The third sort are the thriftless poor, as the rioter who has consumed all his wealth, the vagabond who will stay nowhere but goes from place to place and the rogue who pretends to be ill.

▲ **William Harrison wrote this in 1587 in his book _The Description of England_.**

Acts of Parliament were passed to lay down guidelines for dealing with the poor and the homeless. By the end of Elizabeth's reign more Acts of Parliament had been passed to try to improve the way in which the poor who could not look after themselves were cared for. Some of these acts forced people to give money to their parish authorities for looking after the poor. However individual towns and villages still made their own arrangements for dealing with poor and homeless people.

3.1 Why was poverty a problem in Elizabethan England?

One of the reasons for the increase in numbers of the poor and the vagabonds was because the population as a whole was rising. Another was because the prices of basic goods like bread were rising, whereas wages did not change. There was no real understanding of the relationship between rising prices and low wages, and no awareness of the consequences. The government was not able to make plans to

create more jobs for people since they simply did not know how many people there were in the country at any one time. The first national census was not held until 1801.

The 16th century, in comparison with previous centuries, was a time of few wars between England and foreign countries. This meant that men who had before been employed as soldiers were out of work. Many of these had been **vagabonds** beforehand and

> The poor multiply in numbers because for the most part all the children of the poor are also poor. They are not taken from their wandering parents and brought up to honest labour for their living, but follow the idle steps of their parents. They live and die as most shameless and shameful rogues and beggars.

▲ **William Lambarde tries to explain why the numbers of poor people were increasing. This is taken from a book written in 1594.**

▲ **This woodcut is from a book written in the 16th century by John Taylor. It shows three types of vagabond.**

so had no home to go to. They took to roaming the countryside in search of food and shelter. Henry VII had brought to an end many of the disputes between members of the English nobility which had come to a final crisis in the **Wars of the Roses** in the late 15th century. Noblemen had once kept armies of their own to make sure that they could defend their homes and their lands. Henry VII made this illegal so the soldiers in those private armies often found themselves out of work and with no home. They, too, often took to the roads as vagabonds. The increase of what were called '**sturdy beggars**' forced Henry VIII's government to recognise the difference between those who *could* not work and those who *would* not work. In 1531 an Act of Parliament was passed which stated that the **impotent poor** (those who could not look after themselves) were to be looked after by each parish. The **able-bodied poor**, and the 'rogues and vagabonds' were to be punished.

Elizabeth's government made a further distinction. They realised that some of the able-bodied poor just could not find work. Those who wanted to work but could not were usually called **paupers** and were allowed to receive support from their

parishes. Elizabeth and her ministers were anxious to continue and extend the legislation begun under Henry VIII and Mary I, so as to lead to 'the punishment of rogues' and 'the relief of the poor'. These words are taken from the titles of two Acts of Parliament passed in 1597.

How many vagabonds and paupers were there in Elizabeth's England?

It is impossible to find out exactly how many vagabonds there were. There are no complete or reliable records of their numbers, though there are various accounts from different parts of the country. A Justice of the Peace from Kent, Thomas Harman, wrote a book in 1566 in which he described the different sorts of vagabonds which he had come across. He met an old man who could remember a band of 280 beggars in one Kentish barn in the 1520s. He published a list of 215 male vagabonds who roamed the counties of Essex, Middlesex, Surrey, Sussex and Kent and invited his readers to estimate how many there might be in the whole country. Edward Hext, a Somerset JP, wrote to Lord Burghley in 1596 about the gangs of between 40 and 80 vagabonds who were travelling in his own county.

It is also very difficult to estimate how many paupers there were in the towns and villages. The most detailed records of numbers of paupers come from the larger towns which set up systems for helping the poor during Elizabeth's reign. For example, Norwich made a census of its paupers in 1570. This found that a quarter of the population needed some sort of help in order to feed and clothe themselves.

Why were people afraid of vagabonds?

Villagers and townspeople all over England feared the bands of wandering beggars. Imagine a village in the 16th century, isolated from other villages and a long way from a large town. Travel is difficult and slow. The villages are self contained and the villagers all know each other. They speak in a similar way, using the local dialect. Visitors and strangers are infrequent and cause much interest, bringing news from other parts of the country. The arrival of a band of wandering beggars, however, brings terror. The villagers may not understand what the vagabonds are saying, since they speak in a different dialect. They are afraid they will rob their homes. They may bring disease with them, and disease meant suffering and death, as so little was known about the cause of infection or its treatment. The days of the **bubonic plague** were not yet over. People living in towns were also afraid of bands of wandering beggars. The Bellman (Source E) was there to warn the townspeople that robbers were around.

Elizabeth's government also feared the bands of sturdy beggars. They might provide a very ready source of support for any organised rebellion against the Queen; they might even rebel themselves and cause disorder and fear in the countryside. Such disruption put a

Source D

Almighty God has created all things in heaven and earth in a most excellent and perfect order. In the earth he has set up kings, princes, with other governors under them. He has appointed all people to their duty and order. Some are in high degree, some in low, some kings and princes, some priests, some masters and servants, fathers and children, husbands and wives, rich and poor.

▲ **From a book published in 1547 and written by Sir Thomas Elyot, who was a Member of Parliament during Henry VIII's reign.**

Source E

▲ **This picture is on the title page of a book called *The Belman of London*. The bellman went round the streets calling the time and telling people to beware of robbers.**

SUMMARY

pauper	a poor person who is receiving help from his or her parish
impotent poor	those who were unable to look after themselves: e.g. the sick, the old, orphans
vagabond	a wandering beggar
sturdy beggar and able-bodied beggar	a fit and healthy beggar

Source F

◀ This woodcut, showing a beggar being whipped through the streets, was made in the 16th century.

strain on the whole system of 'keeping the Queen's Peace' and could lead to a partial breakdown of law and order. Whatever the case, these people challenged the accepted social order by not working and taking their place in family and society. They were, therefore, challenging the way in which God had organised the world (Source D). If anyone overthrew this great **'chain of being'** the world, people believed, would end in chaos.

Whatever people believed and feared, Tudor kings and queens had to face up to the problem of poverty and try to do something about it.

SUMMARY

These laws were passed before Elizabeth's reign to try to deal with paupers and vagabonds.

▶ **1531** Able-bodied beggars should be whipped. Those who were disabled could be allowed by JPs to beg, but only in agreed areas.

▶ **1536** Sturdy beggars were to be punished by enforced labour. They were to be hanged if they persisted in begging. Voluntary collections were to be made in parishes to support the disabled poor.

▶ **1547** Sturdy beggars to be made into slaves for two years, or for life if they ran away. All offenders to be branded on the chest with a 'V'. The disabled poor were to be helped by the provision of housing and money, funded by each parish.

▶ **1549** The harsh provisions for sturdy beggars (1547) were abolished. A house was to be set up in every parish where the helpless poor were to be looked after.

▶ **1552** No-one was to sit and beg openly. Local communities were to name two collectors of donations for the poor who would make a collection each Sunday. Those who refused to contribute would be spoken to by the church ministers. Names of the poor and of those who contributed to their support should be recorded.

QUESTIONS

1 Read Source C on page 26. Does this give a good explanation for the rise in the number of the poor in the 16th century? Explain your answer, using the information in this chapter to help you.

2 Read pages 25-6. Explain the *different ways* in which

   a impotent poor
   b vagabonds
   c paupers

   were to be treated.

3 Why was it so difficult to know how many paupers and vagabonds there were in England in the 16th century?

4 Why were the laws dealing with vagabonds so harsh?

When Elizabeth came to the throne punishment for vagabonds was severe, though hanging for persistent begging had been abolished in 1549. The impotent poor were better treated, and laws passed during the reign of Mary I had begun to try to force people to give money to support them. This was reinforced by the first Poor Law passed in Elizabeth's reign, in 1563. There was no change in the harsh treatment of vagabonds, but people who refused to contribute to the relief of the poor were to appear before the Justices of the Peace. If they continued to refuse, they could be imprisoned. Fines were also set out for those who neglected their parish poor-law duties (£2) or refused to act as a collector of money for the poor (£10). **Churchwardens** who did not report those unwilling to serve as collectors were to be fined £20. This was a good deal of money at a time when a skilled craftsman might earn only £7 a year, and shows how important the government felt it was to enforce the laws dealing with the poor.

As Elizabeth's reign went on, people began to recognise and describe the many different sorts of vagabonds who were wandering the country. Some of the able-bodied beggars pretended to be ill in order to beg for money more successfully. (See the box on this page.)

The concern about the numbers of wandering beggars led to a stiffening of penalties in the 1572 'Act for the Punishments of Vagabonds and for the Relief of the Poor and Impotent'. The death penalty was reintroduced for vagabonds who were caught begging twice (unless someone agreed to employ them) and in any case for those who were caught three times. When first arrested a vagabond was to be whipped and a hole burned through the thick part of the right ear, unless an 'honest householder' agreed to give him work.

INFORMATION BOX

The different types of vagabond seen on the roads

Bawdy baskets women pedlars who sold goods from door to door

Demanders for glimmer women who travelled around with false documents which said that they had lost all their goods through fire

Abraham men beggars who pretended to be mad

Palliards or clapperdudgeons men who were born beggars. Some pretended to be ill by making artificial sores on their bodies

Counterfeit cranks beggars pretending to be epileptics. They used soap to make themselves foam at the mouth

Dummerers beggars who pretended to be deaf and dumb

Source A

▲ Nicholas Jennings was an able-bodied gentleman who pretended to be a beggar. This picture shows him as a 'respectable gentleman' on the left, and as a 'counterfeit crank' on the right. It comes from a pamphlet produced early in Elizabeth's reign warning people about vagabonds.

◀ A beggar, in tattered clothing, asks for money from a well-off gentleman. This woodcut appeared in a book written in 1569.

In 1576, an 'Act for the Setting of the Poor on Work, and for the Avoiding of Idleness' began a system of giving work to the impotent poor to do in their own homes. In every town officials were to keep stocks of wool or cotton materials to hand out to the poor to spin and weave. They would be paid for what they did but, if they refused to work, they would be sent to a '**House of Correction**'. These were to be set up in every county, and paid for by the money collected for supporting the poor. For the first time, those people who refused just once to contribute to the cost of poor relief were to be punished. They were to be forced to pay twice the amount they had been asked for in the first place.

When a period of warfare ended many discharged, homeless soldiers and sailors joined the bands of vagabonds roaming the country. They were all the more dangerous since they were trained fighting men. Many had been wounded and were unable to work. After the Spanish Armada of 1588 (see Chapter 5) the fighting with Spain tailed off and ex-soldiers and sailors returned home. An Act of Parliament passed in 1593 made special arrangements for these men. They were to receive a sort of pension in the form of a weekly sum of money paid out by county officials. Each parish in each county was to contribute to this. If, however, an ex-soldier took his pension and still begged he would be punished as a vagabond.

Poor laws of the 1590s

In 1597 a number of laws were passed which laid the foundations for dealing with the poor for the next 240 years. The death penalty for vagabonds was finally abolished, except for any discharged soldiers who were roaming around and committing crimes. Vagabonds were to be whipped, sent to another parish or, if they were persistent beggars, sent overseas to another country.

In the parishes throughout the country 'overseers of the poor' were to be appointed. Their job was to decide how much money was needed for poor relief. They then had to see how much each householder was able to pay and to collect the money. People refusing to contribute to the **poor-rate** could be sent to prison. After that, the overseers were to meet the paupers who asked for help, each week, and decide whether or not they needed help. The impotent poor were to be given relief in the form of money, food or clothing; the able-bodied poor were to be given work to do. Vagabonds were to be punished and sent on their way.

In 1601 Elizabeth's government gathered all the different laws which had been passed in her reign into one Act. You can read part of this Act in Source C.

Source C

Every person which is by this Act declared to be a rogue, vagabond or sturdy beggar, who shall be caught begging, shall be stripped naked from the middle upwards and shall be openly whipped until his body be bloody, and shall be forthwith sent from parish to parish. First of all he shall be sent to the parish where he was born; if this is not known he shall be sent to the parish where he last lived for one year; if this is not known he shall be sent to the parish through which he last passed without punishment.

The poor and impotent people of every parish shall be supported by weekly contributions. This will be collected by collectors in each parish and paid out weekly to the poor since none of these shall openly sit begging. If any member of the parish shall obstinately refuse to pay towards the relief of the poor then the Justices of the Peace at the Quarter Sessions can fine them. If he refuses to pay, he will be sent to prison.

▲ An extract from the Poor Law Act of 1601.

SUMMARY

The Poor Laws passed during Elizabeth's reign

► **1563** The harsh treatment of vagabonds to be continued. The impotent poor were still to be supported, and anyone refusing to pay towards their keep would appear before the JPs. Parish poor-relief officials who neglected their duties would be fined.

► **1572** Death penalty re-introduced for persistent beggars. On first arrest vagabonds would be whipped and a hole burned through their right ear unless someone agreed to give them work.

► **1576** The poor would be given work to do in their own homes. If they refused, they would be sent to a 'House of Correction.' These were to be set up in every county. People refusing to pay the local poor-rate were to be punished.

► **1593** Ex-soldiers would be paid a pension but treated as vagabonds if they begged.

► **1597** Death penalty for vagabonds abolished. They were to be whipped and sent on their way. Overseers of the poor appointed in all parishes to collect and administer poor-relief.

► **1601** All the Poor Laws passed during the reign were put together in one act.

QUESTIONS

1 What changes were made in the ways in which the poor were treated during Elizabeth's reign?

2 Vagabonds continued to be treated harshly. Why was this?

For centuries towns and villages had looked after their own poor without any help from the governments of the time. Even in Elizabeth's reign, when the Queen and her government made more and more laws to deal with the deserving poor as well as vagabonds, local communities continued to look after their own poor. This was mainly because of the age-old belief that true Christians should give help to those less well-off than themselves. They were expected to give money voluntarily to support the poor in their own parishes. Many better-off people took food and clothes to the poor and sick. This helped to keep beggars, who were a nuisance and spread disease, off the streets.

Poor relief in the towns

If a town knew how many poor people it had, and what their needs were, then the officials could plan better to help them. In the late 16th century a number of towns started to make a census of those who were out of work and needing support. The earliest census was held in Norwich in 1570. The names, ages and trades of all the poor in the city were listed. Warwick also started a census of the poor, and you can read part of their 1587 census in Source A. The information was used to decide who needed help and what sort of help these people needed. Children might be sent as apprentices to local tradesmen; the old and the disabled would probably be given relief. A census would help to sort out those who deserved support from those who didn't. For example, after the Warwick census of 1587, only just over half of the 236 poor townspeople were thought to deserve relief. One of the results of holding a census was, therefore, to limit the numbers of people receiving relief. Another method of doing this was to get the poor to wear badges. Without these, they could not receive any relief.

Many towns, including London, Lincoln, Norwich and Ipswich, made plans to set the poor to work. This was even before the 1576 'Act for Setting the Poor on Work' made this compulsory for local authorities throughout the country. Similarly, many towns, including London, Cambridge and Ipswich, set out punishments for those who would not contribute to the poor-rate long before the 1597 Act of Parliament made this compulsory throughout the country.

Source A

Roger Bredon of age 50 years, has a wife 50 years old and a child named Elizabeth. The mother and the daughter beg.

Miles Atown of the age of 60 years, has Isabel his wife aged 48 years; they have four children, Thomas, 10 years; William, 7 years; William the younger, 4 years, and Alice, 6 months old. They all beg.

▲ An extract from the Warwick census of the poor, made in 1587.

Source B

Date	Place	No. of Poor	Poor households	Poor as proportion of total population
1557	Worcester	777	321	18%
1570	Norwich	2359	790	22%
1587	Warwick (one parish)	236	85	12%
1597	Ipswich (nine parishes)	410	120	13%

▲ These figures have been worked out from the censuses of the poor held in these towns.

▲ **These almshouses were built at Hengrave Hall in Suffolk during the reign of Elizabeth 'for the relief and sustenance of ancient servants of the family or poor persons of the village of Hengrave'.**

London, in particular, had to make provision for the large number of poor and homeless people. Many of these came in to the city from other areas. Five institutions were set up to try to keep vagabonds and the impotent poor off the streets. Bridewell was for the able-bodied; Bethlehem or 'Bedlam' for those who were mentally ill; Christ's Hospital for orphans; St Bartholemew's and St Thomas's for the impotent poor and the sick.

Poor relief in the counties

It was more difficult to organise poor relief in the counties. Villages and hamlets were scattered and communications difficult. However, the counties did what they could to solve their problems of poverty. The county of Essex, for example, set and collected a poor-rate as early as 1555. There are records of people in Wiltshire being fined for not paying the poor-rate in the 1580s. There is also evidence that the counties, in particular,

increased poor-relief payments when there were bad harvests, as in 1586 and 1587 and all four years between 1594 and 1597.

Private charity ('alms-giving')

Measures taken by the government and the town and county authorities to deal with the problem of poverty were not, by themselves,

Source **D**

In 1625 Elizabeth endowed the almshouses at Hengrave with £30 or so a year that the poor could live there.

In 1626 she endowed the manor of Lackford with £4 a year to give 12 poor people clothes on All Saints Day every year.

In her will in 1628 Elizabeth left all her servants 40 shillings.

▲ **Some of the charitable donations made by Elizabeth Kytson of Hengrave Hall in Suffolk.**

enough. If rich people had not continued to give money to support the poor, and leave sums of money for the building of '**alms houses**' (see Source C) or hospitals in their wills, there would have been far more people starving and homeless on the streets. In Ipswich, for example, Henry Tooley, a rich merchant, left enough money for houses and a hospital to be built for the poor. An historian, W K Jordan, did a great deal of research in the late 1950s into the gifts made to support the poor in the 16th and 17th centuries. He worked out, from the records which he studied, that about £170,000 was raised in this way between 1560 and 1600, compared with only about £12, 000 through the official poor-rates. These figures may not be completely accurate since not all the records from the time have survived, but they show how important private charity was, even when there was a state system to support the poor.

QUESTIONS

1 There were laws set out for the whole country about how to deal with the poor. Why, then, did individual towns and counties make their own arrangements for their own poor?

2 Why do you think that some people preferred to give money privately to help the poor, even though there was a national system for collecting money for this purpose?

3.4 How far did Elizabeth and her government solve the problems of poverty and vagabondage?

Vagabonds and the able-bodied poor

If solving a problem means making it go away, then Elizabeth did not solve the problem of vagabondage and begging. Much was done through Acts of Parliament and the work of town and county authorities, but numbers of vagabonds increased during and after Elizabeth's reign. The worst problems were in the towns, especially London. In 1582 one of the city officials reported to Lord

Burghley that he had arrested and punished between 200 and 300 vagabonds in London in 10 days. Most, however, were not Londoners. They had come in from as far away as Wales and Somerset. Yet only 15 years later well over half of the vagabonds sent to Bridewell had been born in London. This suggests that numbers of unemployed and homeless people were increasing in London.

Source A

Date	Christ's	Bridewell	St Thomas's	St Bart's	Total
c1560	386	445	243	346	1420
c1580	564	586	737	(580)	2467
c1600	716	899	(700)	(600)	2915
1610	684	1827	998	855	4364
1634	1032	1380	1143	1181	4736

▲ Admissions to the London institutions for the poor, c1560 – 1634. Figures in brackets are estimates, since the records are either missing or have big gaps in them.

Sending vagabonds to Bridewell kept them off the streets, but this did not prevent people from becoming wandering beggars in the first place. Sending them from place to place, as the 1601 Act laid down (see Source C, page 31), did not solve the problem. It just passed it on from one village or town to another. More laws were passed during the 17th century to try to deal with vagabonds. This suggests that the problem had by no means been solved: there were just different ways of trying to cope with the situation.

Setting the poor to work

This was an idea which continued well into the next three centuries, though this did not, again, reduce the numbers of the able-bodied poor nor did it increase the number of jobs in the trades and industries. Neither central nor local government knew how many jobs were available. They just assumed that there were jobs for all. Unlike governments in this century they did not have statistics to help them to plan for making jobs available in areas of high unemployment.

The population as a whole was rising, as you read in Chapter 1. This made everything more expensive because there were more people wanting the same number of goods, or the same amount of food, as when the population was smaller. Since the government was not aware that the population was rising, there were no plans to increase output. To make things worse, wages did not rise to take account of the rising prices. In years of bad harvests, as in the four years between 1594 and 1598, the Privy Council brought in more grain from abroad, and arranged for food to be taken from better-off areas to those worst hit. But this was response to a crisis rather than long-term planning. It was caused, for example, by local authorities reporting that whole families as well as individuals were asking for relief from their parishes.

The deserving poor

Many better-off people believed that being poor was a punishment for being sinful or lazy. They did not approve of handing out money to the poor, especially when they had to provide the money. This partly explains why the poor-rate was made compulsory by the end of Elizabeth's reign. Another reason for this was the rising number of deserving, 'impotent' poor, especially in the towns. London can again provide an example of this. Numbers admitted to the five institutions which had been founded grew during Elizabeth's reign and after (see Source A).

Elizabeth I did not manage to stop people from taking to the roads as vagabonds, or needing poor relief from their parishes. She did not succeed in making every area of the country treat the poor in the same way, though the poor laws which were passed during her reign went a long way towards doing this. The mixture of laws, private charity and the efforts of town and county authorities combined to contain the situation. Bands of wandering beggars did not rise up in revolt against local communities or the government, even if their numbers went up. The poor were looked after, as far as possible, in their own towns and villages, though their numbers, too, went up. The laws for the relief of the deserving poor and for the punishment of vagabonds, passed in 1597 and finalised in 1601, remained virtually unchanged until 1834. Of course it was one thing for Parliament to pass the laws, but that did not mean that they were always obeyed.

QUESTIONS

1 What does Source A tell us about the different sorts of poor people who were taken into these institutions between 1560 and 1634? Use the information on pages 33 and 34 to help you with your answer.

2 Why was it made compulsory for people to contribute to the poor-rate by the end of Elizabeth's reign?

Source 1

The Tudor policy of dealing with poverty and vagrancy had two main aims: to punish and deter the vagrants and to relieve the 'deserving poor'.

In both cases, history books written some time ago concentrate on the laws passed to deal with the problems, as though new measures were not tried until Parliament had passed acts, which were then immediately enforced throughout the country.

Yet Acts of Parliament are a poor guide to what actually happened. Charitable individuals, JPs and town councils did much in advance of national legislation. Indeed they often provided the example and inspiration for that legislation.

It is equally true that unpopular laws were often not enforced, despite the threats of the Privy Council.

▲ **From a book written in 1983 by the historian D M Palliser about England between 1547 and 1603.**

Source 2

The problem of the poor was twofold. There were those who could not work and those who would not work; so, at least, contemporaries saw it, and there is really precious little evidence that those who wanted work but could not find it ever made up a sizeable proportion of the wandering poor.

After the beginnings of a planned poor law in 1536, various Acts of Parliament gradually made up a general system for providing charity, work and punishments. This system was brought together in two great Acts, in 1597 and 1601, summing up the Elizabethan poor law.

As the century drew on the problem became manageable, and the Elizabethan poor law proved satisfactory until the greater upheaval of the late eighteenth century raised entirely new difficulties.

▲ **From a book written in 1955 by the historian GR Elton about Tudor England.**

1 Read Sources 1, 2 and 3.

Source 1 says that
'...history books written some time ago concentrate on the laws passed to deal with the problems, as though new measures were not tried until Parliament had passed Acts, which were then immediately enforced throughout the country.'

a Read Source 2, which was written in 1955. Is Source 1 right about what Elton says?

b Read Source 3, which was written in 1874. Is Source 1 right about what Green says?

c Does what you have read in Chapter 3 lead you to agree or disagree with the judgement in Source 1 that '...Acts of Parliament are a poor guide to what actually happened'?

2 To what extent did Elizabeth solve the problems of poverty and vagabondage? Why was she unable to remove these problems completely?

Source 3

The opening of Elizabeth's reign saw her face the social difficulty which had so long held up British progress. The solution to the problem lay in the system of poor laws.

▲ **From A Short History of the English People, written in 1874 by the historian JR Green.**

CHAPTER 4

PAPISTS AND PURITANS: RELIGION IN ELIZABETHAN ENGLAND

During the reign of Elizabeth I's grandfather, Henry VII (1485 – 1509) the people of England, like those of all other countries in Western Europe, were Roman Catholic. They accepted the Pope as the leader of the Catholic Church and they accepted everything which they had been taught by the Church to believe. Change followed under Elizabeth's father, Henry VIII, who brought to an end the Pope's authority over the Church in England. During the reign of his son, Edward VI, the Church started to adopt some of the changes in religious beliefs from the continent. People who accepted these new ideas about religion became known as Protestants.

1553 – Catholic restoration

Elizabeth's sister, Mary I, who reigned between 1553 and 1558, was devoutly Catholic. She was determined to restore the Pope's authority over the Church in England, and make England officially Catholic again. She also married the powerful – and unswervingly Catholic – king of Spain, Philip II. However, the changes which had been taking place over the previous 20 years meant that some people in England resisted the move back to Catholicism. About 300 of those who resisted – both clergymen and ordinary people – were burned alive. A number of Protestant clergymen went abroad to the Netherlands and parts of Germany, where their new beliefs were accepted and practised.

1558 – Catholic or Protestant?

When Elizabeth came to the throne in 1558 she had to make a decision, quickly. Should England remain Catholic or move back towards the Protestantism which had developed during her father's and her brother's reigns? The decision could not be made in isolation, it was inevitably going to be influenced by England's relationships with other countries.

The Catholic king Philip of Spain had been married to her sister, Queen Mary. The Queen of Scotland, Mary (who was Elizabeth's cousin) was Catholic, and married to the Catholic heir to the French throne. England had supported Spain in a war against France since the last year of Mary's reign. Philip II was anxious to bring this war to an end. He hoped that this would be done with English help. Elizabeth also had to take account of her own beliefs and feelings and those of her own people who were not, by any means, united.

Source A

During the Christmas festivities at Court there had been a good deal of merrymaking which made fun of the cardinals and bishops of the Catholic Church. This had been allowable in the officially Protestant Court of Edward VI. Elizabeth's position was more delicate. Philip of Spain had proposed marriage to his sister-in-law Elizabeth and, with the peace negotiations with France still in progress, Elizabeth could not afford to offend him.

▲ The historian Maria Perry writing in 1990 describes people's feelings about religion soon after the start of Elizabeth's reign.

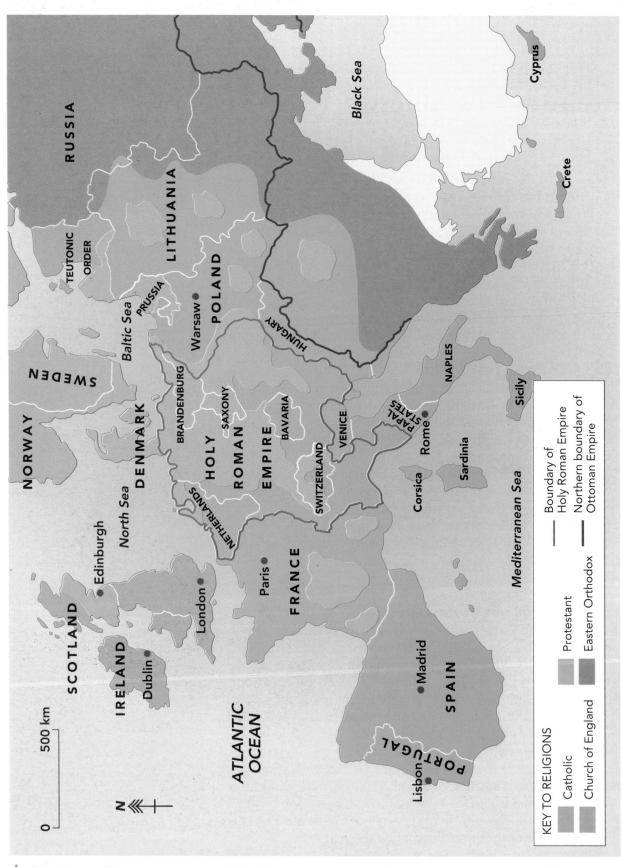

KEY TO RELIGIONS

Catholic	Protestant
Church of England	Eastern Orthodox

Boundary of
Holy Roman Empire

Northern boundary of
Ottoman Empire

▲ The religions of European countries in 1558.

For most people in Elizabeth's England, whether they were Catholic or Protestant, religion was a centrally important part of their lives. The church was the place where townspeople or villagers met to pray together and to worship God. Religion provided the explanation, comfort and help for all the ups and downs of everyday life, and death. The 'will of God' was responsible. This was a time when many children died at an early age. Illnesses from which, today, virtually everyone recovers, like appendicitis and influenza, often resulted in death.

In the 16th century those about to die, and those who were left behind, were comforted by their belief that the souls of the dead could go to heaven to live with God forever. They knew, however, that some people's souls would go to hell rather than heaven. The horrors of hell were well illustrated in churches and constantly described by priests. Praying to God was one way of trying to stop people's souls from going to hell.

After the **Reformation**, Catholics and Protestants came to believe in different reasons for people going to heaven or hell. For some Protestants, including those who followed the teachings of John Calvin, it all depended on whether God had chosen people to be saved from hell even before they were born. For other Protestants, especially those who followed the teachings of Martin Luther, it all came down to whether their faith and belief in God was enough to make them live the sort of life which would allow them to be saved.

For Catholics, being saved from hell depended on people receiving God's 'grace' continually throughout their lives to help them to be good. This involved receiving what are called the '**sacraments**' of the church, for example being baptised and taking **Holy Communion**. These different beliefs lay at the heart of the importance which religion had for people. They also lay at the very centre of the disagreements between Catholics and Protestants.

SUMMARY

Religious changes in England 1534 – 1558

▶ **1534** The English Parliament passes an Act which makes Henry VIII Supreme Head of the Church in England.

▶ **1536-39** Henry VIII's Parliament orders that all monasteries in England should be closed and their wealth transferred to the Crown.

▶ **1547-53** England becomes Protestant under Edward VI.

▶ **1549** The first Prayer Book in English is to be used in all churches.

▶ **1553** Mary I starts bringing England back to Catholicism under the Pope.

▶ **1555-58** Mary I burns over 300 Protestants.

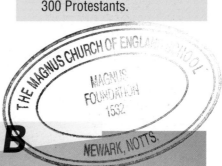

Source B

The most important moment of Catholic worship was collective: a congregation united in worship at the moment when the priest elevated the consecrated bread.

The most important moment of Protestant worship was utterly lonely: the worshipper alone before God, looking into his own soul to ask whether his faith was sufficient, and hoping he knew the answer.

▲ **The historian Conrad Russell wrote this in an article published in 1988.**

QUESTION

1 What problems did Elizabeth have to face when deciding on the future of religion in her country?

Elizabeth came to the throne on 17 November 1558. In January 1559 Parliament met to discuss the arrangements by which Elizabeth and her ministers proposed to settle religious affairs in England. By May the decisions had been made and Parliament had passed the Acts which made up Elizabeth's religious settlement. The fact that the religious settlement had been discussed and decided so early in her reign shows how important Elizabeth and her ministers felt this to be.

The way in which the religious settlement was carried out through Acts of Parliament followed the pattern set by Elizabeth's father, Henry VIII, her brother, Edward VI and her sister, Mary I. This meant that the structure of the English Church was laid down by law and so anyone who did anything contrary to this law would be punished. It also meant that Elizabeth was continuing with her father's policy that any future changes to the religion of England would also have to be made through Parliament.

Elizabeth's aims

Elizabeth wanted this settlement to set down the official rules of how the Church of England was to be governed and how church services should be carried out. Her most urgent aim was to ensure that the country was as unified as possible in its religious beliefs and practices. She knew that a country divided in such an important matter as religion would be open to conflict at home between Protestants and Catholics. Then it only needed a strong Catholic country like Spain to support English Catholics for there to be serious trouble – even civil war.

Philip II of Spain suggested marriage to Elizabeth in the hope of continued English support against France. Elizabeth, however, had no intention of agreeing to this, even for the sake of avoiding trouble with Spain. On the other hand, Elizabeth was alarmed at the number of Protestant **exiles** who returned from Europe as soon as her sister, Mary, died. She did not want her country to be under the influence of extreme Protestants any more than she wanted it to stay Catholic. She rejected the idea of the Pope having any power over the Church in England but neither did she want plain, simple **Puritan** church services.

The Acts of Parliament which made up Elizabeth's religious settlement first and foremost separated the English Church once again from the power of the Pope. These acts were the Act of Supremacy and the Act of

Source A

A woman in Christ's Church is not called to be an apostle, a leader, a teacher or preacher. Therefore she cannot be supreme head of Christ's Church on earth, nor of any part thereof.

▲ Archbishop Heath speaks his mind to the House of Lords on Elizabeth becoming head of the English Church in March 1559.

Source B

All and every archbishop, bishop and all and every other ecclesiastical person shall make, take and receive an oath...
'I, [name] do utterly testify and declare in my conscience, that the Queen's Highness is the only Supreme Governor of this realm, as well in all spiritual things as temporal, and that no foreign prince or person has or ought to have any power or authority ecclesiastical or spiritual within this realm, and I do promise that from henceforth I shall bear faith and true allegiance to the Queen's Highness.'

▲ Adapted from the Act of Supremacy, March 1559.

Uniformity. They also set up a framework for defining what people should believe about central religious issues like the sacraments and how church services were to be carried out. They were not entirely successful in preventing people from staying with their long-held Catholic beliefs. Some areas in the north of England remained firmly Catholic.

The Act of Supremacy

The Act of Supremacy became law on 8 May 1559. There were no problems getting it through the House of Commons, but in the Lords all the bishops voted against it, though it still passed, by 33 votes to 12. The bishops, all of whom had been appointed by Mary I, objected to separating England from the power of the Papacy. They also found it difficult to accept that the Queen should follow her father and brother and become Supreme Head of the Church in England. You can read the views of Nicholas Heath, Archbishop of York, on this in Source A. The solution was to call the Queen 'Supreme Governor' rather than 'Supreme Head', though this did not satisfy the Catholic bishops who remained firm in their support for Papal Supremacy.

The Act of Supremacy required all clergymen and government officers to take an **Oath of Supremacy** (Source B). By this they were to swear that they would accept Elizabeth as Supreme Governor. In 1563 this oath was extended to schoolmasters, lawyers and Members of Parliament.

The Act of Uniformity

The Act of Uniformity (May 1559) laid down rules about the religious services which were to be carried out in churches throughout the country. Two of the most important aspects of this concerned the sacrament of Holy Communion and the clothes (known as vestments) which a priest (or minister, as Protestants preferred to call him) should wear during the services. In the reign of Edward VI a prayer book in English was produced in 1549 to replace the Latin service book which had always been used before. In this prayer book, when the priest gave Holy Communion to the people the words which he used reflected the Catholic belief that the bread had actually become the Body of Jesus Christ during the part of the service known as the '**consecration**'. Protestants throughout Europe had rejected this belief in the 'real presence' of Christ's body in the bread and the wine.

A second prayer book, produced in 1552, showed a much more Protestant bias. The words which the minister was to use reflected the Protestant belief that the service of Holy Communion was no more than a memorial to Christ's death. However, the Book of Common Prayer produced in 1559 and

SUMMARY

The Elizabethan Religious Settlement

Changes

► The Pope has no power in England. Elizabeth is Supreme Governor.

► Services and the Bible to be in English. Prayer Book combines Catholic and Protestant beliefs.

► All but one of Mary's Catholic bishops dismissed.

Continuity

► Clergy to wear traditional vestments.

► Many parish clergy remain taking the Oath of Supremacy.

► Changes carried out by Act of Parliament as they had been under Henry VIII and Edward VI.

Source C

'The Body of our Lord Jesus Christ, which was given for thee, preserve thy body and soul unto everlasting life. Take and eat this in remembrance that Christ died for thee, and feed on Him in thy heart by faith with thanksgiving.'

'The Blood of our Lord Jesus Christ, which was shed for thee, preserve thy body and soul unto everlasting life. Drink this in remembrance that Christ's Blood was shed for thee, and be thankful.'

▲ **From the Book of Common Prayer, 1559.**

authorised by the Act of Uniformity combined the two different beliefs about the nature of the bread and the wine (Source C). Thus Elizabeth hoped that both Catholics and Protestants might feel comfortable with the words which they heard and so believe what they wished without breaking the law.

The 'Vestiarian Controversy'

An Act of Parliament passed in 1549 during Edward VI's reign had required clergy to wear traditional vestments. A further Act, passed in 1552, was much more Protestant and allowed clergy to wear only a simple black gown and white **surplice** for services. Traditional vestments were then restored by Mary I. A decision clearly had to be made. Elizabeth firmly believed that clergymen should wear traditional vestments and this very much influenced the final decision that ornaments and vestments should be as they were in the second year of the Edward VI, 1548. Protestants returning from exile in Europe after Mary's death were disappointed. They saw these traditional vestments as signs of 'Popery'. Soon some began to ignore the official rules about vestments and wore only a gown and surplice for church services.

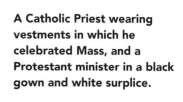

A Catholic Priest wearing vestments in which he celebrated Mass, and a Protestant minister in a black gown and white surplice.

The Settlement is enforced

Elizabeth's first Parliament ended on 8 May 1559. By the beginnning of June she and her advisers were ready to put the religious settlement into operation. They had already put together a series of rules, or **injunctions**, about how clergy should conduct both religious services and their private lives. Though Elizabeth privately disapproved of clergymen marrying, she did not prevent this, as the Catholic Church did. The royal injunctions allowed clergy to marry but only after the lady in question, who should be 'honest and sober', had been examined by the bishop and two JPs. The injunctions also laid down that the Bible should be placed in every church. Three or four men in each parish were appointed to keep a check on people's attendance at church services, and take note of Catholic-minded people who might be absent.

Source D

Article 25: It is a thing plainly against the Word of God to have public Prayer in the Church, or to minister the Sacraments, in a language not understood by the people.

Article 27: Transubstantiation cannot be proved in the Holy Bible, but is against the plain words of Scripture and has given rise to many superstitions. The Body of Christ is given, taken and eaten, only after a heavenly and spiritual manner.

Article 37: The Bishop of Rome has no power of law in this Realm of England.

▲ **Adapted from the Thirty-nine Articles, 1563.**

The Oath of Supremacy was administered by a new court called the Court of High Commission. Of all the bishops which Mary I had appointed, only the Bishop of Llandaff in Wales took the oath. Only a very small number of ordinary clergy refused to take the oath. Those who refused were dismissed from their posts. This meant that, whilst there was very little change in the parish churches throughout the country, Elizabeth could replace the Catholic bishops with men who would, she hoped, support her settlement and bring stability to the Church of England.

One of her most important appointments was Matthew Parker, a Cambridge-educated priest in favour of moderate religious reform. He was a close friend of William Cecil. Mary I had dismissed Parker as Dean of Lincoln in 1554 and he lived in hiding until Elizabeth came to the throne. He was made Archbishop of Canterbury in 1559. Until his death in 1575 Parker supported the spirit of Elizabeth's settlement by trying to limit the spread of extreme protestantism.

The Thirty-nine Articles

One of Archbishop Parker's first responsibilities was, together with the other bishops and archbishops, to define the teachings, or doctrine, of the Church of England. They based their work on the Forty-two Articles which Archbishop Cranmer had put together in 1553, in Edward VI's reign. The Thirty-nine Articles, published in 1563, formed the basis of religious teaching in the Church of England for over 350 years. They still contain the official doctrine of the Church of England and can be found in the Book of Common Prayer which still exists today. These Articles rejected Catholic teachings, particularly about the power of the Pope and the 'real presence' of Christ in the bread and wine taken at Communion (Source D).

By 1563, Elizabeth's religious settlement was complete. She had no wish to see things change further, and hoped that people of all variations of belief could worship and live together within the Church of England.

▲ **Matthew Parker, Archbishop of Canterbury.**

For Protestants who had come from abroad the Church of England was still too Catholic, but for those who had never changed their Catholic beliefs the Church of England was Protestant. Elizabeth had brought about a rapid change from the Catholicism which her sister Mary had set up to a Church of England which looked back to both Henry VIII's and Edward VI's reigns. Moreover, this had taken place without open opposition as had arisen in France. The question was, could Elizabeth's settlement continue to survive the opposition of both strong Catholics and strong Protestants?

QUESTIONS

1 What were the main decisions about religion made in

  a the Act of Supremacy and
  b the Act of Uniformity?

2 Why were the clothes worn by clergymen in church services so important to Protestants?

3 Was Elizabeth's religious settlement a complete change from the past? Explain your answer.

The first challenge to Elizabeth's religious settlement came from those who wished that the Church of England had moved much further away than it had from the beliefs and practices of the Catholic Church. Elizabeth herself had never wanted to insist that everyone should hold the same beliefs about, for example, the nature of the bread and the wine during the service of Holy Communion. She did, however, want all services in all churches to follow the 1559 Prayer Book, whatever people were thinking or believing during the services. Many Protestant reformers wanted to go further than this. They wanted 'popish' vestments, crucifixes and statues of the Virgin Mary and the saints to be removed, by order of the law, from all churches. Elizabeth was not prepared to go this far.

The Puritans: who were they?

Those who wanted more extreme Protestant reforms became known as 'Puritans'. The historian Patrick Collinson has described Puritans as 'the hotter sort of Protestant'. They wanted to 'purify' the Church of England by returning to the simple and uncomplicated worship and way of life of the earliest Christians. They followed the teachings of the New Testament closely and believed that the rituals, ceremonies and teachings which had been developed over the centuries by the Catholic Church went against God's original intentions for his people. These were set down in the Bible and could not be changed. They wanted the heart of every church service to be the minister preaching to the people, teaching them God's word. Different Puritans, however, wanted to achieve reform in different ways. John Jewel, Bishop of Salisbury, for example, wanted moderate reform, but extreme reformers like Richard Cox and Henry Barrow wanted to change the organisation of the Church of England along the lines of Swiss and German reformed churches.

Challenge came, first of all, in Convocation, the Church's equivalent of Parliament. The ordinary clergy who met in the Lower House of Convocation put forward demands for change in 1563 (Source A). These proposals were defeated by only one vote. This showed the strength of feeling in favour of reform amongst the ordinary clergy.

Source A

That in all parish churches the minister in common prayer turn his face toward the people, and there distinctly read the divine service appointed.

That in baptism the ceremony of making the Cross on the child's forehead be omitted as tending to superstition.

That since some communicants are not able to kneel during the time of communion because of age or sickness, that whether they kneel or not be left to the decision of the minister in charge.

That it be sufficient for the minister when saying divine service to use a surplice.

That the use of organs be removed.

▲ Adapted from the Puritan demands in the Lower House of Convocation, 1563.

Source B

Some say the service by the altar, others in the body of the church; some say in a surplice, others without a surplice; the table standeth in the body of the church in some places, in others it standeth in the middle of the chancel; in some places the table standeth upon trestles; in some places the table has a carpet, in others it has not; administration of Communion is done by some with surplice and cap, some with surplice alone, others with none; some receive Communion kneeling, others standing, others sitting; some baptise infants with the sign of the cross, others not.

▲ Adapted from the returns of a survey of religious practice in England, submitted to William Cecil in 1564.

How unified was the Church of England?

A survey of religious practices in English parishes, carried out by William Cecil in 1564, showed that the Act of Uniformity had not been particularly successful (Source B). The Queen was not pleased. She wrote to Archbishop Parker in January 1565 expressing her displeasure at such lack of uniformity (Source C). The Archbishop did his best to deal with these problems. In 1566 he issued a series of 'Advertisements', or recommendations for how clergy should conduct services (Source D). In these he urged that there should be no differences in the ways in which different clergymen carried out church services. For Puritan clergy the issue of vestments, in particular, remained a problem about which they continued to rebel despite the Archbishop's 'Advertisements'.

To preach or not to preach?

The royal injunctions of 1559 had insisted that all clergy should preach one sermon a month. This should teach the congregation how to live a godly life. Few parish clergymen, however, had the knowledge or the ability to do this effectively. The large number of these who had been Catholic parish priests had been required only to say the services laid down first of all in the Catholic service book and then in the English Prayer Book. The Catholic tradition did not demand the ability to teach congregations, through preaching, how they should live a godly life according to God's laws. Catholics believed that whenever the priest administered sacraments like baptism and holy communion, he was giving people help and support from God to enable them to live as they should. Bishop Grindal of London, who later became Archbishop of York, and then of Canterbury, supported those who believed in the importance of preaching and educating clergy so that they could do this effectively.

Source C

We thought, until this present, that these errors, tending to breed splits in the church, should have been stopped. But perceiving that they begin to increase we have determined to have all such errors reformed and repressed. We do by this letter charge you to confer with the bishops and make them understand what varieties and diversities there are in our clergy, and proceed by order of such laws as are provided by Act of Parliament.

▲ Elizabeth wrote this letter to Archbishop Parker on 25 January 1565.

Source D

The Queen's Majesty, remembering how necessary it is to the advancement of God's glory for all her loving subjects to be together in unity of doctrine and uniformity of church services has charged that some order might be taken whereby all differences might be reformed. These orders and rules have been thought right to be used and followed:

That no parson, not admitted by the bishop of the diocese to preach, do preach in his own church or anywhere any scripture or doctrine, but only read the teachings already set out in the Book of Common Prayer.
That every minister saying public prayers or ministering the sacraments shall wear a surplice with sleeves, to be provided at the charges of the parish, and that the parish shall provide a decent table standing on a frame for a communion table.
That all communicants do receive communion kneeling.

▲ Adapted from Archbishop Parker's 'Advertisements', or recommendations for order in the Church of England, 1566.

QUESTIONS

1 What does the word 'Puritan' mean?

2 What did the Puritans want to achieve?

3 What evidence do Sources B, C and D provide of lack of uniformity within the Church of England?

4 Why was preaching so important to Protestants but not to Catholics?

Presbyterianism and Prophesyings

In 1570 Thomas Cartwright, who taught theology (the study of religion) at Cambridge University, started a serious challenge to the religious settlement. He claimed that his study of the New Testament showed that it was wrong to govern the church through its existing system of bishops and archbishops. The early Christian Church was organised through 'elders', chosen from and so representing each community. Cartwright argued that this was how the Church of England should be organised. There should be committees of elders representing individual parishes. These should send men to a national committee which represented the different parts of the country. This was how Calvin's Church in Geneva was run, and it was how Scottish Protestants wanted their church to be organised. The Queen and some of her advisers saw this as a direct challenge to the Royal Supremacy and the power of the bishops and archbishops within the church. Cartwright was dismissed and had to flee to Europe.

Cartwright had, however, set a ball rolling which could not be stopped. His views appealed to many Puritans who saw government of the church through bishops and archbishops as a relic of 'Popery'. Cartwright's teachings led to the development of 'Presbyterianism' in England (the Greek word for 'elder' is 'presbyteros'). His views were attractive to many members of the House of Commons who also preferred a Presbyterian approach to the organisation of the Church of England.

In 1571 the MP William Strickland introduced a bill into the Commons to change the Prayer Book along Puritan lines. Elizabeth promptly banned the Commons from bringing in bills to do with religion until they had been discussed by the bishops. Undeterred, Presbyterian sympathisers delivered two documents, called 'Admonitions' to the Commons (Source E). These did not result in any changes. Puritans tried printing and issuing pamphlets critical of the government's religious policies. Elizabeth hit back by issuing an order to control the printing presses.

Prophesyings

Puritans who valued good preaching above the services laid down in the Prayer Book were also beginning to challenge the religious settlement. Groups of clergymen began to meet together to hear sermons from good

Source E

The outward marks whereby a true Christian church is known are preaching of the word purely, ministering the sacraments sincerely, and ecclesiastical discipline.

Firstly popish massmongers, King Henry's priests, King Edward's priests, Queen Mary's priests should be utterly removed.

Appoint to every congregation a learned and diligent preacher.

Remove articles and injunctions.

Take away the lordship, the pomp and the idleness of bishops.

▲ Adapted from the Puritans' 'Admonitions to Parliament', 1572.

Source F

▲ John Whitgift, Archbishop of Canterbury.

preachers and discuss them afterwards. These meetings were called 'prophesyings', a term used in the New Testament to describe similar meetings held in the early years of the Christian Church. Elizabeth saw these meetings as dangerous and against the laws set down to govern the Church of England. As such, they threatened her position as Supreme Governor of the Church of England.

Matthew Parker, after years of trying, without success, to suppress Puritanism, died in 1575. He was replaced by Edmund Grindal, the Archbishop of York. Elizabeth ordered Grindal to suppress these 'prophesyings'. Grindal was far more in sympathy with Puritan ideas than Parker had ever been and was most unhappy about the Queen's order. He saw the 'prophesyings' as a way of improving the standard of preaching in the church and refused to suppress them. Elizabeth immediately suspended him from his post as Archbishop of Canterbury. He remained suspended until his death in 1583.

John Whitgift

Presbyterianism and Prophesyings grew and flourished until Archbishop Grindal died in 1583. Elizabeth was then able to appoint as Archbishop of Canterbury a man much more in tune with her own views. John Whitgift, a Cambridge scholar and teacher, supported the Queen's views on the organisation of the church. He decided to hit out at those who would not conform with the laws of the religious settlement. In 1583 Whitgift produced Three Articles (Source G) which were enforced on the clergy by the Court of High Commission which had been set up in 1559. Clergymen who could not agree with the Articles were dismissed from their posts. People either had to stay with the Church of England and accept its rules or leave to join the separate, independent churches which were beginning to be set up. Most stayed within the Church of England.

Though the Puritan movement had, for the moment, been weakened as a force within the Church of England, Elizabeth and her advisers were still determined to deal with the 'break-away' churches. In 1593 three leaders of these churches, Robert Browne, Henry Barrow and John Greenwood were executed for treason. Elizabeth had always believed that there must be uniformity within the Church of England. Challenge from within the country, as from those who set up independent churches, threatened this uniformity – and Elizabeth's authority over the Church – and must be dealt with firmly.

By the end of Elizabeth's reign Puritanism, though contained, was by no means dead. Many people at all levels of society supported the further reform of the Church of England. They hoped that Elizabeth's successor would be willing and able to do this.

Source G

All clergy must agree that:

1 Her Majesty, under God, has the sovereignty and rule over all persons born in her realms.

2 The Book of Common Prayer shall be used and none other.

3 The Book of Thirty-nine Articles shall be followed.

▲ Archbishop Whitgift's Three Articles, 1583.

QUESTIONS

1 How did Puritans such as Thomas Cartwright think the church should be organised?

2 Why were 'prophesyings'

   a popular with Puritans
   b seen as dangerous by Elizabeth I?

3 Many people supported the changes to the Church of England which Puritans wanted. Why did they not succeed in making these changes?

4 In what ways did Puritans threaten Elizabeth's religious settlement?

The Puritans' challenge to Elizabeth's religious settlement was very much home-based. Though some Protestant clergy in England had links with reformers in Europe there were no strong Protestant rulers who could pose any sort of a threat to Elizabeth if she did not agree to make the Church of England more Protestant. The possible threat from Catholic countries was, however, a different matter. The map on page 38 shows how England was virtually surrounded by Catholic countries. However, the war against France in which England had supported Spain came to an end in 1559. This meant that France and Spain, uncertain that the peace would last, both hoped for friendship with England.

Mary Stuart had been Queen of Scotland since the death of her father, James V, in 1542 when she was only a few months old. She was married when very young to Francis, heir to the French throne. Francis became King of France in 1559 but died only two years later. In 1561, therefore, Mary returned to Scotland as Queen of Scotland and widow of a King of France. She was Catholic. The family tree on page 6-7 shows that she had the best claim to the throne of England, should Elizabeth die without children.

The way in which Elizabeth treated English Catholics could, therefore, have a crucial effect on the way in which foreign Catholic powers behaved towards her and her country. Philip of Spain, however, had no desire to see Mary of Queen of Scots on the thrones of both England and Scotland. The prospect of the Scottish Queen, who had strong links with France, ruling England as well could pose a severe threat to his position as ruler of the Netherlands. The Netherlands, with many centres of trade and commerce, had once brought in a good deal of money to Philip. Throughout his reign, Philip was desperately short of money and was now finding it very expensive to keep hold of the Netherlands. However, Protestantism was growing in the Netherlands and Philip needed to be able to move freely, by land and sea, to keep it in check. He was determined, whatever the cost, to keep the Netherlands under Spanish control. A friendly England would help to secure his sea-routes whilst a friendly, or at least neutral, France would help

Source A

From the very beginning of her reign she has treated all religious questions with so much caution and incredible prudence that she seems both to protect the Catholic religion and at the same time not entirely condemn the new Reformation.

In my opinion, this is a very prudent action, intended to keep control of supporters of both beliefs, for the less she ruffles them at the beginning of her reign the more easily she will keep them in check at the end.

▲ The Imperial Ambassador writes to the Emperor Ferdinand I in March 1559.

▲ The figures on the rood-loft were Christ on the Cross, Mary, his mother, and John, one of his followers. Rood-lofts were built at the top of the archway leading to the choir stalls and altar.

safeguard his land routes. It was against this background, combined with her own desire for religious unity, that Elizabeth tolerated the survival of Catholicism in her country. This was supported from the late 1570s by English Catholics trained as priests abroad. At the start of her reign Elizabeth really did seem to want to avoid making hard-and-fast decisions about whether the Church in England should be Catholic or Protestant. She hoped that people could believe as they wished but worship according to her laws and so remain loyal subjects. The ambassador to the **Holy Roman Empire** approved of this policy (Source A).

The survival of Catholicism in England

As you read in the previous section, Elizabeth was far from achieving her desire for uniformity in religion across the country. Though most of the clergy took the Oath of Supremacy, the newly-appointed Protestant bishops very soon discovered that there was a good deal of Catholic ceremonial still being carried out in parish churches throughout the land (Source B). There were reasons for this. There had been so many changes in religion since the reign of Henry VIII that many clergymen were not convinced that Elizabeth's religious settlement would be final. They were, therefore, reluctant to throw out things like crucifixes and statues. Many of the parish clergy also found it difficult to change beliefs which they had previously held. They could not become Protestant just

because Parliament ordered this. Catholicism remained strong in many parts of the north of England, particularly Lancashire and parts of Yorkshire. It also survived in some areas in the south, as Source B shows. People who refused to give up being Catholic were known as **recusants**.

Most people, however, attended services in their parish churches on Sundays whether or not they liked the changes brought by the 1559 Prayer Book. There was, after all, a fine of one shilling (a good daily wage) if people did not attend church. That was quite a lot of money for ordinary people to pay. Better-off Catholics could afford to pay the fine but Elizabeth and her advisers did not want to come down too hard on people like this, since Catholic gentry often played important parts in local government. During the 1560s, therefore, little was done to enforce the rules of church attendance. The Catholic gentry continued to attend **mass**, usually celebrated in their own big country houses (Source C).

Source C

There be certain families thought to have masses in their houses, which come very seldom or not at all to church. I must confess that I am not able to reform these people without your support.

▲ **From a letter to the Privy Council by Bishop John Scory of Hereford, October 1564.**

Source B

They have still in the diocese, in many places, statues hidden up and other popish ornaments, ready to set up the mass again within 24 hours' warning. Many bring to church the old popish Latin service book. In some places the rood lofts still stand, and those taken down still lie in the churches ready to be put up again.

▲ **From a report written by Bishop Barlow of Chichester in 1569.**

QUESTION

1 Explain the various different reasons which lay behind Elizabeth's decision not to treat English Catholics harshly during the 1560s.

You could look at the various things which influenced her decisions, for example relationships with foreign countries, her own views, and the feelings of English Catholics.

The Northern Rebellion and the Papal Bull

Elizabeth had hoped that catholicism might just die out in England, but her hopes were dealt two fatal blows. First was the rebellion of the Northern Earls in 1569 (see Chapter 6). These Catholic noblemen led an armed rebellion to try to put Mary Queen of Scots on the throne instead of Elizabeth. This showed the strength of Catholic feeling in the north. The second blow was the decision by Pope Pius V in 1570 to issue a **Papal Bull** (order) declaring that Elizabeth was a **heretic**. As such, she was **excommunicated**. No English Catholic, therefore, should accept her as Queen or obey her laws (Source D). This was an explosive situation which could ruin Elizabeth's hopes of a peaceful religious settlement as well as endanger her relationships with foreign Catholic countries.

However, though the Papal Bull is thought to have been issued to co-incide with the rebellion of the Northern Earls (see page 71), this was over by the time news of the Bull arrived in England. The Pope had been relying on English Catholics to support the Bull, but he took no steps to ensure this. He knew that he could not rely on Spain or France to help enforce the Bull since they were too taken up by their own problems: Spain was trying to crush a rebellion in the Netherlands against Spanish rule and French Protestants were beginning to challenge the Catholic French king.

The effect of the Papal Bull

The Papal Bull therefore, was a disastrous mistake. Elizabeth had been right in believing that English Catholics would prefer to keep quiet about their religious beliefs and remain loyal to her. The Pope had seriously overestimated his power over English Catholics. They wanted to continue to live and worship as Catholics but most did not want the Pope to have any political power in England. Now the Bull placed English Catholics in a difficult position. If they obeyed the Bull they risked being charged with treason; if they ignored the Bull they

Source D

Elizabeth, the pretended Queen of England, the servant of wickedness, having seized on the kingdom and monstrously taken the place of Supreme Head of the Church in all England, hath reduced the kingdom into a miserable condition, which was so lately taken back to the Catholic faith and a thriving condition.

Out of the fullness of Our power we declare Elizabeth as being a heretic and to have suffered the sentence of excommunication, and to be cut off from the unity of the Body of Christ. And moreover We do declare her to be deprived of her pretended title to the kingdom of England, and that the nobility, subjects and people of the kingdom be for ever released from all manner of duty and obedience to her.

▲ Adapted from the Papal Bull issued in 1570.

risked excommunication from the Church. In reality, Catholics who ignored the Bull were in little danger of excommunication since the Bull had not been put into effect in England. Even so, Parliament passed a series of Acts in 1571 to protect Elizabeth from any consequences of the Papal Bull.

- Treason Acts made it treason for anyone to say or write that Elizabeth was not the true Queen of England.
- A further act made it illegal for anyone to bring any Papal Bull into England and to carry out its orders.

Both Houses of Parliament agreed a bill which would increase penalties for Catholics who refused to attend Church of England services. Elizabeth, however, refused to give this bill her royal assent. She continued to believe that it was better to try to keep the loyalty of English Catholics than to treat them harshly and risk losing them.

Missionary priests and Jesuits

Elizabeth's 'softly, softly' approach was successful for some time. Most English Catholics had not been significantly affected by the rebellion of the Northern Earls or by the Papal Bull of 1570. In the late 1570s, however, there was a new and much more serious threat to religious peace in England.

William Allen, a Catholic priest from Lancashire, left England in the early 1560s when it was clear that England would not remain Catholic. In 1568, in Douai in the Netherlands, he founded a training college for Englishmen who would later return to England as Catholic priests. In 1574 the first of these priests arrived in England.

The mission of these priests was to help restore England to the Catholic faith. This was dangerous. The Act of 1571 made it illegal for anyone to carry out the orders of a Papal Bull. Anyone, therefore, who tried to persuade English people to accept the authority of the Pope risked being accused of treason, since this would be breaking the law. Apart from frightening the government, little was achieved during the 1570s by the **missionary priests**.

From 1580 onwards, however, they were joined by members of the Society of Jesus, known as **Jesuits**. The Society of Jesus had been founded in 1534 by Ignatius Loyola, a Spanish ex-soldier, to fight against those who rejected the teachings of the Catholic Church. Jesuits were well-educated and trained specifically to bring people back to Catholicism and to support Catholics who could not attend mass officially. Two of the most important English-born Jesuits who came back to England in the 1580s were Edmund Campion and Robert Parsons. Elizabeth knew about the arrival of any Catholic priests in England. One of her government ministers, Francis Walsingham, had a very efficient spy network which kept him, and the Queen, well informed. The priests were forced to hide.

This was usually in the houses of the Catholic gentry. Despite careful precautions priests were often caught and tried for treason. Those who were caught were tortured to try to get information from them about other priests. They were then executed as traitors.

Source **E**

I was born in such time when holy mass was in great reverence, and brought up in this faith. In King Edward's time this reverence was neglected. In Queen Mary's time, it was restored with much applause. And now in this time it pleases the state to question those who continue as Catholics. I hold still to that wherein I was born and bred; and so by the grace of God I will live and die in it.

▲ An unknown Catholic lady explains her reasons for remaining Catholic. This was recorded in the biography, written in the 16th century, of Jane Dormer, an English aristocrat.

Source **F**

▲ Photograph of a 'priest hole', where Catholic priests hid to avoid capture. This one is in Moseley Old Hall, Staffordshire.

Edmund Campion

Father Edmund Campion was a Jesuit priest who came to England in 1580. He stayed for some time in Lancashire, where many people still kept to the Catholic faith. He was eventually caught and imprisoned in the Tower of London. He was tortured and executed on 1 December 1581.

Father Campion believed that he was carrying out God's will in coming to England to try to bring people back to the Catholic Church. Elizabeth's government declared that Campion, an Englishman, was a traitor. He was breaking the law of the land and putting into effect the wishes of the Pope, as expressed in the Papal Bull of 1570. Priests like Campion further believed that they were being persecuted simply because of their religious beliefs. The government, however, always maintained that Catholic priests were being punished as traitors. Read Campion's own words in Source G. He saw himself as a religious reformer, not as a political activist. Now read Lord Burghley's thoughts in Source H. Burghley clearly saw this 'persecution' as punishment for treason. Whatever the reason, Campion was tortured and killed.

English Catholics now faced pressure to reject the Pope's authority over the English Church. During the 1580s, those who were suspected of having anything to do with the Jesuits, and those who gave any cause for concern, could be faced with answering the so-called 'Bloody Questions'. (Source K). The answers given by Henry Orton and John Hart show how they dealt in different ways with the agonising decision faced by English Catholics: could they be loyal subjects and at the same time good Catholics?

In 1581 the fines for not attending Church of England services were raised. In 1585 any Catholic priest could be accused of treason. Fears of Catholic activity against Elizabeth increased in the 1580s because relationships between England and Spain grew worse (see Chapter 5). Ordinary Catholics faced death if they hid priests in their houses.

More than a hundred priests were condemned to death for treason. They had supported English Catholics but had not, despite the government's fears, encouraged rebellion against the Queen. William Allen (Source L) might have encouraged English Catholics to get rid of Elizabeth, but it was never likely that the vast majority would be anything but loyal to their Queen.

Source G

Threats come to us daily, yet we have escaped so far. I have set down in writing the causes of my coming here; that I was a priest, and wished to teach the gospel and minister the sacraments.

I never had mind, and am strictly forbidden, to deal in any respect with matters of State or Policy of this Realm.

▲ Edmund Campion describes some of his feelings about his mission to England.

Source H

There are many people in this realm that differ in some opinions of religion from the Church of England, but they do also profess loyalty and obedience to Her Majesty. None of these are prosecuted or charged with any crimes of treason.

▲ Lord Burghley explains that those who accept the Queen's authority, even if they do not accept the Church of England, are not charged with treason.

Source I

The clergymen they succeed in capturing are treated with a variety of terrible tortures. They drive iron nails between the nails and the quick. Campion, of the Society of Jesus, was tortured in this way. Their fingers and toes were turned black but they did not confess anything under this torture.

▲ Adapted from a Spanish account of English persecution of Catholic priests.

By the end of Elizabeth's reign Catholics were no longer a real threat to the security of the realm. It was estimated that in 1603 there were about 8,500 Catholics who refused to attend the services of the Church of England but over 100,000 Catholics who attended church occasionally to avoid the huge fines.

Source J

▶ An engraving of a Catholic being stretched with weights while his torturers wait for a confession.

Source K

Q *Whether the Bull of Pius V against the Queen's Majesty ought to be obeyed by the subjects of England?*

Orton: Her Majesty was and is to be obeyed by every one of her subjects.
Hart: It is a difficult question that I cannot answer.

Q *Whether the Pope has power to say that any of her Majesty's subjects should not have allegiance to her?*

Orton: I think that the Pope has no such power.
Hart: I say that I have not decided, and so cannot answer.

Q *If the Pope or anyone else, by his authority, invades this realm, which part would you take, or which part ought a good subject of England to take?*

Orton: I say that I would take part with her Majesty against the Pope or anyone else invading the realm.
Hart: I say that when such a case happens, I will then make up my mind.

▲ Some of the responses made by two English Catholics to the 'Bloody Questions'.

Source L

William Allen urges Philip II to undertake his enterprise against England. The Catholics are all clamouring for him, and he urges him to crown his glorious efforts in the holy cause of Christ by punishing Elizabeth, hated of God and man, and restoring the country to its ancient glory.

▲ From a description of a letter written to Philip II of Spain, urging him to invade England.

QUESTIONS

1 How far did the Papal Bull of 1570 pose a real threat to Elizabeth?

2 Explain
   a why priests like Edmund Campion were accused of treason;
   b what Father Campion might have said in his defence against a charge of treason.

3 List the measures taken in the 1580s to make sure that Catholics stayed loyal to Elizabeth.

4 Read Source K. In what ways do Orton and Hart give different answers?

5 Do you think it was possible to be a good Catholic and a loyal English subject?

Elizabeth's religious settlement is complicated and complex. In order to try to understand it we need to look at:

1 the problems facing Elizabeth when she came to the throne;
2 the reasons for her decisions about the religious settlement;
3 the effects of the settlement on Catholics and Protestants;
4 the ways in which Elizabeth and her government dealt with these effects; and
5 whether the settlement fulfilled Elizabeth's aims.

1 Look back at sections 4.1 and 4.2.

   a Describe the situation Elizabeth inherited when she became Queen after the religious changes made during the reigns of Henry VIII, Edward VI and Mary I
   b How did relationships with
      • Spain
      • France
      • Scotland affect the situation?
   c How did the following factors influence Elizabeth's decisions about the religious settlement
      • her own religious beliefs
      • Protestant exiles returning from Europe
      • the fact that all the archbishops and bishops (who had a vote in the House of Lords) had been appointed by her sister, Mary I and were Catholics
      • the fact that her sister sister, Mary I, had been married to Philip II of Spain (see Source 1)?

2 Look back at sections 4.2 and 4.3.

   How did the extreme Protestants, known as Puritans, react to Elizabeth's religious settlement?

3 Look back at section 4.4.

   How did Catholics

   a at home
   b abroad

   react to Elizabeth's religious settlement?

4 Look again at sections 4.3 and 4.4.

   Explain, in as much detail as you can, how Elizabeth and her government reacted to
   a Puritan
   b Catholic response to her religious settlement.

Problems facing Elizabeth when she came to the throne.

Reasons for Elizabeth's decisions about the religious settlement.

The Religious Settlement

Reactions to the Religious Settlement
a Protestants

b Catholics

The Response of Elizabeth and her Government to
a Protestants

b Catholics

▲ King Philip II of Spain (reigned 1556–98) by Antonio Moro, about 1580.

5 Copy the diagram and use the answers which you have made to Questions 1 – 4 to help you complete it.

6 Finally, try to answer these questions in as much detail as you can:

   a Which group provided the greater threat, Protestants or Catholics?
   b Did Elizabeth I succeed in making a lasting religious settlement which satisfied all her people?

CHAPTER 5

ENGLAND, EUROPE AND THE WORLD

When Elizabeth became Queen in 1558 England and Spain were united in war against France. England and France had been enemies for hundreds of years. They had often gone to war with each other. England and Spain had been allies since Henry VIII's reign and war against France began during the reign of Elizabeth's sister, Mary, who was married to Philip II, King of Spain. King Henry II of France supported the claim of his daughter-in-law, Mary Queen of Scots, to the English throne. When Henry II died in 1559 his son Francis became King of France. His wife was now Queen of both Scotland and France. With the prospect of France and Scotland, in alliance, squeezing England between them it was absolutely crucial for Elizabeth to remain on good terms with Philip of Spain. This did not, however, prevent her from refusing his offer of marriage.

In the 1570s, however, Elizabeth seemed to be thinking about marriage with a French prince: first with Henry, Duke of Anjou and then with his younger brother, Francis, Duke of Alençon. They were both sons of Henry II of France. In 1588 the **Spanish Armada** sailed against England. This led to a war with Spain which lasted, on and off, until 1604. England was supported in this by France and Scotland.

Friends with Spain? or France?

This turn-around in relationships in Europe had four main causes.

- Firstly the Netherlands, ruled by Spain but important for English trade, revolted against Spanish rule. Elizabeth helped the rebels against their Spanish rulers, at first in secret. In 1585, however, she sent open support in the form of an army led by the Earl of Leicester.
- Secondly, Spain increasingly supported the Catholic priests who went as missionaries to England.
- Thirdly, John Hawkins, Francis Drake and other English sea-captains refused to accept Spanish domination of the countries of the New World. They attacked Spanish treasure ships – and Elizabeth did not try to stop them.
- Fourthly, France was suffering from civil war between Protestant and Catholic nobles and so posed no threat, for the time being, to England.

Source A

England was involved on the one side with the Scottish, and on the other side with the French war; overcharged with debt brought about by Henry VIII and Edward VI; Calais lost; people having different opinions in religion; the Queen lacking powerful friends.

▲ William Camden sums up Elizabeth's situation in 1558, in a book published in the early 17th century.

Source B

The French King tried to persuade the Pope to declare Elizabeth a heretic and illegitimate. The King of Spain tried to prevent this. The French King determined to claim England for his son and daughter-in-law Mary Queen of Scots. He ordered that they should use the title, Francis and Mary by the grace of God, King and Queen of Scotland, England and Ireland.

▲ William Camden describes the French claim to the English throne through Mary Queen of Scots.

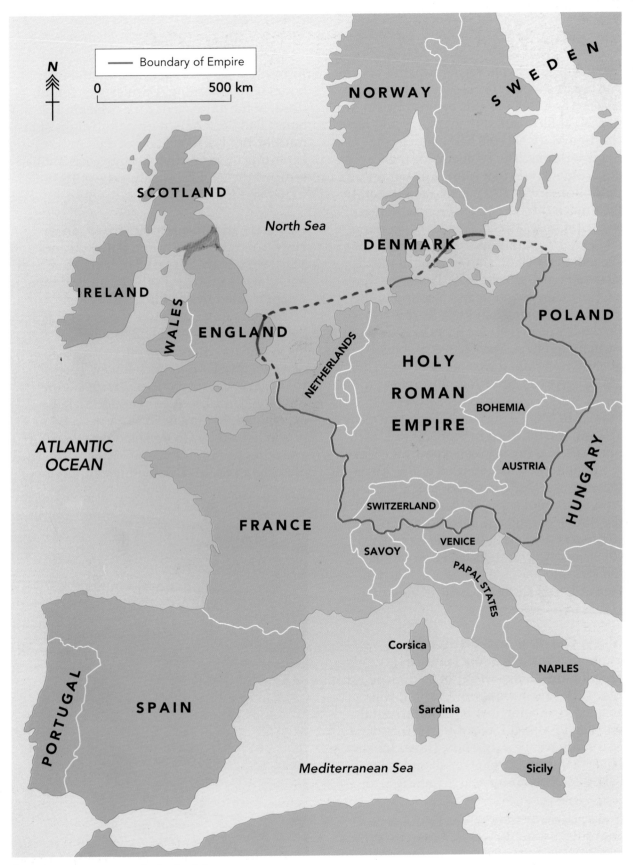

▲ **Europe in the reign of Elizabeth I.**

Mary Queen of Scots was Elizabeth's cousin. She became Queen of Scotland when her father was killed in battle against the English in 1542. If Elizabeth did not marry and have children Mary had the best claim to the English throne. The problem, for the English government, was that Mary was not only Catholic but was also married to the heir to the French throne. Mary's French mother, Mary of Guise, acted as regent of Scotland whilst her daughter was in France. A Protestant rebellion started in Scotland against French rule in 1559. This was supported by England and resulted in the Treaty of Edinburgh in 1560. By this treaty England was to help the Scots to get rid of the French. In return, Mary Queen of Scots was to give up her claim to be Queen of England. Mary, however, never formally agreed to this.

Francis II, Mary's husband, died at an early age and she returned to Scotland in 1561. Elizabeth and her advisers knew that Mary would marry again and tried to find the right man for her. The 'right man' meant someone who would not support Mary in her claim to the throne of England. Elizabeth even suggested the Earl of Leicester as a husband (Mary rejected him). In 1565 Mary took matters into her own hands and married Henry, Lord Darnley, a great-grandson of Henry VII.

Mary, Darnley and Bothwell

Mary gave birth to a son, James, in June 1566. Despite this, things were not going well for Mary. Her husband, Lord Darnley, was suspected of being involved in the brutal murder, in March 1566, of a favourite of Mary's, her Italian secretary, David Rizzio. Later that year, Darnley fell ill and went to Kirk o'Field, a house near Edinburgh, to

▶ Mary Queen of Scots, painted by an unknown artist in 1558 when she was 16. At the time she was married to the heir to the French throne and was living in France.

recover. On 10 February, 1567, in the early hours of the morning, Darnley was found, dead, in the gardens of Kirk o' Field. The house had been blown up on the night of his murder, but Darnley had not died in the explosion. It seems that he and a servant had escaped the explosion only to be quickly found and killed.

Very soon after this Mary married James Hepburn, Earl of Bothwell. Bothwell and Mary were both suspected of being involved in Darnley's murder. Bothwell and his men were defeated by the forces of Scottish Protestant nobles who wanted to get rid of both Mary and Bothwell. Bothwell fled after his defeat and Mary was put in prison in a castle on an island in Loch Leven. Later in 1567 Mary was forced to **abdicate** and her little son, James, was crowned King James VI of Scotland. In May, 1568 Mary escaped from prison helped by George Douglas, the young and attractive brother of Sir William, the Lord of Loch Leven. Mary joined her supporters,

Source A

but they were defeated by Scottish government forces at Langside, near Glasgow. Mary fled to England, hoping for support from her cousin, Elizabeth I. She arrived at Workington Hall, Cumbria on 16 May, 1568.

Mary in England

Mary's arrival in England posed a problem for Elizabeth which she was to find very difficult to resolve. Elizabeth believed that it was wrong to support those who rebelled against their lawful monarch, as the Scots had done. If Elizabeth supported rebellion against a fellow monarch, she would logically be supporting the idea that it was right to rebel against *any* monarch – including herself. So she could not send Mary back as a prisoner to those who had rebelled against her: this would be saying that she agreed with what they had done. Neither could she send Mary back to Scotland with English support for her claim to be Queen of Scotland again, or even to be regent for her son, James. This would mean that Mary could reinforce her claim to the *English* throne, probably with French help. And if Mary stayed in England she could become the focus of Catholic plots against Elizabeth. The only answer was to let Mary stay in England, but as a royal prisoner in 'honourable captivity', that is, kept in custody but treated with the respect due to a Queen.

Murder? 'Not proven'

However, Mary still had to face the difficulties that Darnley's death had created. She was put on trial in 1568. Letters between Mary and Bothwell were produced by the Scottish **regent**, Murray, which were supposed to show that Mary had been Bothwell's mistress before Darnley's murder, and that she had been involved in his murder. These letters are known as the '**Casket Letters**' since they had apparently been found in a silver casket taken from one of Bothwell's personal servants earlier in 1568. These letters have never, to this day, been proved to be either true or false. Early in 1569 the case against Mary was declared

'not proven'. Mary then began almost twenty years of 'honourable imprisonment' in various English castles.

Plots against Elizabeth

The Rebellion of the Northern Earls which began in 1569, the year after Mary arrived in England (see pages 71-2), was enough to convince many of Elizabeth's advisers that Mary's presence in England, even as a prisoner, was dangerous. This was made worse when Roberto di Ridolfi was accused, in 1571, of plotting against Elizabeth. Ridolfi was an Italian Catholic banker who had worked in London but was now back in Europe. Cecil and Walsingham found that he had been trying to organise Mary's marriage to the Duke of Norfolk, a Catholic English noble, as part of a plan to put Mary on the English throne and restore Catholicism. Norfolk was arrested, found guilty of treason and executed in 1572.

In 1583 Mary was again accused of being involved in another plot against Elizabeth. In 1582 Walsingham heard rumours of a conspiracy which involved some Scottish

Source B

Darnley almost at once turned out to be unsatisfactory both as a husband and also as a king. Drunken, idle and arrogant he neglected government business, angered the nobles and put his wife against him.

▲ The historian Penry Williams gives his judgement about Darnley, *The Later Tudors*, 1995.

Source C

Mary was much ill-treated by her ungrateful subjects, deposed from the throne and driven into England. She was thrust forward to dangerous undertakings by Englishmen who wanted to restore the Romish religion.

▲ William Camden, writing at the beginning of the 17th century, gives his view of Mary Queen of Scots.

▲ The execution of Mary, Queen of Scots.

Jesuits, the Spanish ambassador, Mendoza, and Mary. He then discovered that the link between these was Francis Throckmorton, an English Catholic.

Throckmorton was arrested and confessed, under torture, that there was a plot in which France and Spain would invade England, release Mary and make her Queen of England. Throckmorton was executed and Mary was moved to Chartley, Staffordshire, where she would be watched closely by a strict Puritan, Sir Amias Paulet.

Mary's execution

In 1586 Walsingham declared that he had discovered a plot, involving Mary, to assassinate Elizabeth. His agents discovered letters from Antony Babington, a young English Catholic, to Mary, offering to kill Elizabeth. Mary's reply was also found, which seemed to approve of the plan. Elizabeth reluctantly signed her death warrant and Mary was executed in February 1587. When Elizabeth heard that Mary had been executed she was desperately upset. She blamed a junior Secretary of State, William Davison, for misunderstanding her orders.

QUESTIONS

1 What reasons might Mary have had for being involved in Darnley's murder?

2 What problems did Mary's arrival in England pose for Elizabeth?

3 Is it fair to say that Mary was responsible for the three plots against Elizabeth between 1571 and 1586? Explain your answer.

4 Why, in the end, was Elizabeth so upset about Mary's execution?

5 How would you sum up Mary Queen of Scots as a person? Use all the evidence which you have to produce no more than two or three sentences. Make sure you support your conclusions with evidence.

SUMMARY

Important events – England and Scotland

▶ **1559** Mary Stuart, Queen of Scots becomes Queen of France.

▶ **1560** Treaty of Edinburgh.
Death of Mary's husband Francis II of France.

▶ **1561** Mary returns to Scotland.

▶ **1565** Mary marries Henry, Lord Darnley.

▶ **1566** David Rizzio, Mary's secretary, murdered.

▶ **1567** Darnley murdered. Mary marries Bothwell.
Bothwell defeated. Mary abdicates.

▶ **1568** Mary flees to England, and is put on trial.

▶ **1569** Rebellion of the Northern Earls.

▶ **1571** The Ridolfi Plot.

▶ **1583** The Throckmorton Plot.

▶ **1586** The Babington Plot. Mary tried and found guilty of treason.

▶ **1587** Mary Queen of Scots executed.

Only a year before Elizabeth became Queen in 1558, Mary I, Elizabeth's sister, lost Calais to France. This was during the war which Spain and England were waging against France. Calais was the last remaining part of the French empire over which English monarchs had ruled since the days of the Norman and Plantagenet kings. In many ways the loss of Calais was a relief, since England no longer had to try to keep any sort of control over even a very small part of France. On the other hand it meant that France now controlled the whole of the coastline opposite England. England could no longer keep a check, from both sides, on who sailed up the Channel.

In 1559 the Treaty of Cateau-Cambrésis brought an end to the war against France. Three months after the treaty was signed Francis II became King of France. He was married to Mary Stuart, Queen of Scotland. In 1560 Francis II died and his widow returned to Scotland. By this time, as you have read, the Scottish Protestant nobles, with English help, had forced the French to leave the country.

Civil war in France

In 1562 civil war broke out in France between Catholics and Protestants. Now that French influence in Scotland had been removed Elizabeth felt able to send help to the French Protestants without fear of the Scots and the French getting together against her. Elizabeth's main reason for sending help was not because she wanted to support Protestantism. It was mainly because she wanted to regain a foothold in France to protect the seaways to and from the south of England. Her plan didn't work. England gained Le Havre, a northern French port, in 1562 in return for support for the Protestants, but lost it again the next year.

For a while, relations with France were quiet. In 1568 England and Spain fell out with each other. Elizabeth took possession of a large shipment of gold and silver when Spanish ships took refuge in English ports against French Protestant pirates. In the same year Mary Queen of Scots arrived in England. In 1569 the rebellion of the Northern Earls (see pages 71-2) showed that English Catholics were prepared to support Mary's claim to the English throne. Elizabeth realised that she needed an ally in Europe.

Will Elizabeth marry a French Prince?

The most obvious choice was France, and the best way of forging an alliance was through marriage negotiations. These were started in 1570 between Elizabeth and Henry, Duke of Anjou the brother of the young King Charles IX of France. The Treaty of Blois between England and France was agreed in 1572, but there was, in the end, no marriage with the

Source A

You and your husband shall have such strength in France that the French King shall not be able, or shall not dare, to attempt anything against you. You shall be able to protect the Protestants of France against the Papists. You shall be able to force the King of Spain to treat his subjects in the Low Countries well.

▲ The Earl of Sussex describes the advantages of a French marriage in a letter to the Queen, 1578.

Source B

Her Majesty's age, being about 45 years may give doubt as to whether she can bear a child. If she does not, the realm must put up with her husband for the rest of her life, with no successor. The Duke of Alençon, on the Queen's death, might then marry the Queen of Scots, so that he can enjoy England and Scotland.

▲ Lord Burghley gives his reasons for opposing a French marriage, 1579.

▲ **The Protestant Henry of Navarre who became King Henry IV of France in 1589.**

SUMMARY

Important events – England and France

▶ **1559** Treaty of Cateau-Cambrésis brings the war against France to an end.

Francis II, husband of Mary Queen of Scots, becomes King of France.

▶ **1560** Death of Francis II of France.

▶ **1562** England agrees to help French Protestants in return for Le Havre.

▶ **1563** French religious wars become worse. England loses Le Havre.

▶ **1570** Elizabeth considers marriage with the Duke of Anjou.

▶ **1572** Treaty of Blois.

Elizabeth begins marriage negotiations with the Duke of Alençon.

▶ **1579** Elizabeth again pursues marriage with the Duke of Alençon.

▶ **1581** Alençon arrives in England to finalise the marriage arrangements (unsuccessfully).

▶ **1584** Death of the Duke of Alençon. The Protestant Henry of Navarre becomes heir to the French throne.

▶ **1589** Murder of the Catholic Henry III of France. Henry of Navarre becomes king, supported by England.

fiercely Catholic Duke. The negotiations had, however, served to keep France friendly during the problems caused by the Ridolfi Plot. In 1573 Elizabeth began marriage negotiations with the youngest brother of the French King, the Duke of Alençon. Nothing happened. It was not until 1579 that the courtship was revived. By this time the Duke of Anjou had become King Henry III of France and both England and France felt threatened by the way in which Spain was regaining control of the rebellious Netherlands.

The idea of marriage with the Duke of Alençon was not popular in England. John Stubbs, a Puritan gentleman, published an attack on the marriage proposals. He was punished by having his right hand chopped off, though he did shout 'God save the Queen', before he passed out. In the end, Stubbs lost his right hand for no reason. The marriage negotiations floundered and in 1584 Alençon died. The heir to the French throne was now the Protestant Henry of Navarre. In 1589, Henry III of France was murdered and Henry of Navarre became king, supported by England. From then until nearly the end of Elizabeth's reign she supported Henry IV, even to the extent of sending troops to help him against Spain.

QUESTIONS

1 Read Sources A and B.
   a What *advantages* does the Earl of Sussex see in a French marriage?
   b What *disadvantages* does Lord Burghley see in a French marriage?
   c Was Burghley being more realistic than Sussex about the results of a marriage for Elizabeth? Explain your answer.

2 How serious do you think Elizabeth was about marrying either the Duke of Anjou or the Duke of Alençon?

It wasn't until Henry VIII's reign that the different parts of Spain came together to form a strong country which could challenge the rest of western Europe. England and Spain were on good terms and Elizabeth's relationship with Spain, England's old ally, began well but grew worse even during the first 10 years of her reign. Philip II of Spain had no desire to see Mary Queen of Scots as Queen of England and so supported Elizabeth until it was no longer possible for him to do so. You read, on page 61, about the main reasons for changes in the relationship between England and Spain. We will now look in more depth at why the situation became so bad that England and Spain ended up at war with each other.

The Netherlands

Revolt against Spanish rule in the Netherlands began in the 1560s. Elizabeth had to be careful about taking sides. On the one hand, England depended on trading centres in the Netherlands to sell English cloth. On the other hand she still needed Spanish friendship. Problems began when, in 1563, Margaret of Parma, Philip II's regent in the Netherlands, stopped English traders from sending cloth to the Netherlands to be sold in Antwerp. This was mainly to get back at England for the attacks by English pirates on Spanish ships in the Channel. It was also because she hoped that a block on English trade would help Spanish trade.

The stoppage of trade lasted only until 1565, but there was worse to follow. In 1566 there were widespread riots in Antwerp and other Netherland cities against Spanish rule. In 1567 Philip II sent the Duke of Alva to the Netherlands with an army which was to destroy all opposition. Some of this opposition was from Protestants. English traders were also suffering under Alva's increasing control of the Netherlands. Alva now had huge forces stationed over the Channel only 30 miles from the English coast.

Source A

▲ William, Prince of Orange. His rather twisted expression is because he was wounded in the face during an assassination attempt in 1582.

Soon, however, Protestants in the Netherlands were to be united under William, Prince of Orange, in an area which they later called the United Provinces. For how long could Elizabeth stop herself from sending support to William of Orange?

England sends an army to the Netherlands

Elizabeth had no desire to help rebels against their ruler, but she realised that Alva's activities posed a threat to England. She tried to get the best of both worlds by not openly falling out with Spain but, at the same time, allowing the 'Sea Beggars' (Protestant pirates from the Netherlands) to use English harbours. At the same time she encouraged English sea-captains like John Hawkins to trade with areas such as Central and South America which Spain claimed as its own.

▲ Portrait of Francis Drake, painted between 1580 and 1585 by an unknown artist.

Source C

The Queen, my Sovereign Lady, has ordered me to come to these parts. If it is wrong it is she who knows best and I am not to be blamed for anything whatsoever. I do not want to gain anything which belongs to anyone but King Philip. I do not want the people in this country to pay for what I might take. But I am not going to stop until I have collected the two millions that my cousin, John Hawkins, lost at San Juan de Ulua.

▲ Francis Drake argues that he will try to avenge the Spanish attack on Hawkins at San Juan de Ulua in 1568.

When Elizabeth seized Spanish ships in 1568 Alva responded by seizing English property in Antwerp. However, Philip could not afford a war against England any more than Elizabeth could afford a war against Spain. It wasn't until the early 1580s that the situation became really serious. Philip II of Spain had now also become King of Portugal. This gave him extra money and a powerful navy. He could now challenge the English at sea.

In 1584 William of Orange asked the Duke of Alençon to become first Protector and then Sovereign of the United Provinces. Alençon's attempts at this were useless. Later that year William of Orange and the Duke of Alençon, heir to the French throne, both died. The Catholic faction in France drew closer to Catholic Spain since the next heir to the French throne was the Protestant Henry of Navarre. Protestants in the Netherlands hoped that Elizabeth would help them against the Spanish. She was reluctant, but in the end she agreed. In 1585 the Earl of Leicester was sent to the Netherlands with an army of 7,600 men. This amounted to a declaration of war against Spain.

English pirates in the New World

The civilisations of the American-Indian people of Central and South America are at least as old as those of western Europe. Yet we often refer to these people and their countries in the 16th century as 'the New World'. This is because, before European voyages across the Atlantic at the end of the 15th century, the peoples of these two parts of the world knew nothing about each other. By Elizabeth's reign, however, Spain had a huge empire in the West Indies and Central and South America.

The English only started to claim land in the Americas under Elizabeth, and during the first 30 or so years of her reign, English seamen were either slave-traders or pirates. Both these activities threatened Spanish domination of the New World and contributed to the worsening of English relationships with Spain.

San Juan de Ulua

In 1562 John Hawkins began to take people from the west coast of Africa to the West Indies and Central America. He sold them for a high price as slaves to the Spanish settlers in these areas. The Spanish officials in the Caribbean generally chose to ignore Hawkins' activities and welcomed the chance to buy slaves. In 1568, however, Hawkins was forced to shelter in the harbour of San Juan de Ulua in Mexico. He had already sold almost 500 people as slaves. At this point the Spanish treasure fleet arrived. The commander did not approve of Hawkins' slave dealing in Spanish waters and ordered his men to attack the English ships. Three were sunk. The rest arrived back in England without most of the money made from slave dealing. Hawkins gave up the slave trade but San Juan de Ulua was not forgotten.

In the years between the San Juan de Ulua disaster in 1568 and the defeat of the Spanish Armada in 1588 Francis Drake and his fellow English sea-captains took every opportunity to attack Spanish treasure ships in the Caribbean. The Queen did not give her official approval for this. On the other hand she did not forbid the activities of these English pirates. In 1581 Elizabeth knighted Francis Drake on board his ship *The Golden Hind* , showing that she approved of what Drake had achieved.

Would English Catholics have supported a foreign Catholic invasion?

Elizabeth and her government were continually worried about the activities of Jesuits and other priests who came into England to try to support English Catholics. As relations with Spain worsened so the government put pressure on Catholics to reject the Pope's authority, and Catholic priests were punished as traitors. The support given by Spain to these missionary priests certainly fuelled Elizabeth's anger against Philip II. This was, however, no more blame-worthy than the support which Elizabeth gave to the Protestants in the Netherlands. Both Elizabeth and Philip were, quite naturally, anxious to defend their own lands.

We have very little evidence that any of Elizabeth's Catholic subjects would have supported an invasion of England to re-establish Catholicism. Most people wanted to remain loyal to Elizabeth, even if they attended Catholic services in secret. We have evidence that Cardinal William Allen tried to persuade Philip II to invade England (see page 53). Allen was, it seems, to have played a big part in returning England to Catholicism, and in the new Catholic state after the successful invasion. His part is explained in notes sent from the King to his commander in the Netherlands, a month before the Armada sailed for England.

Source D

The principal reason which has moved his Majesty to undertake this enterprise is his desire to serve God, and to convert to His Church many peoples who are now kept down by the enemies of our Holy Catholic faith.

▲ The Duke of Medina Sidonia wrote this shortly before the Armada sailed, in his orders to his Spanish troops.

Source E

The complete conquest of England was unlikely, since it would have involved a long campaign for which the Spanish army was inadequately supplied. Yet, once in military occupation of Kent, Parma could have dictated terms to a Queen who, in any case, wanted peace. She might have been forced to abandon her Dutch allies.

▲ The historian Penry Williams explains what Philip II was hoping to achieve.

The Spanish Armada

The arrival of English troops in the Netherlands and the activities of English sea-captains in Spanish-American waters were too much for Philip II. He prepared plans for an invasion of England. These plans were leaked to England and, in April 1587, Sir Francis Drake sailed for Cadiz, Spain. He destroyed all the ships in the harbour. These were, however, not ships which Philip would have used in any invasion by sea. What was far more important was that Drake went on to the Azores, west of Spain in the Atlantic. There he captured a Spanish ship the *San Felipe*, which had a cargo worth some £140,000 (probably many millions today). The Spanish sea-captain Santa Cruz, who was to be the commander of the invasion fleet, was immediately ordered to follow Drake and protect other Spanish ships in the area. This meant that the Spanish Armada was not ready to sail until 1588. The English government, therefore, had more time to prepare its defences.

The Armada sails for England

The Spanish fleet finally sailed in July 1588. Santa Cruz had died in February 1588. The new commander, the Duke of Medina Sidonia, was to call in to Calais on his way up the Channel to take on board soldiers from the army of the Duke of Parma, Philip II's commander who was, at the time, recovering territory for Spain in the southern Netherlands.

Source F

The Spanish fleet consisted of 65 first-line galleons and an equal number of smaller ships. It carried 18,000 troops and 7,000 sailors. 17,000 of Parma's troops were to be picked up to land in England.

The English navy roughly matched the Spanish in ships. Elizabeth contributed 34 ships, of which 19 were over 200 tons, and mobilized a further 30 armed merchant ships, together with many smaller ones. In size the English ships were as big as the Spanish and were somewhat easier to handle. The great difference lay in the guns. The English were almost certainly stronger in short-range, medium and long range guns than the Spanish. The only weapons in which they were weaker than the Spanish were lightweight weapons which were of little effect in naval warfare.

The Spanish land forces were, by contrast, undoubtedly stronger.

▲ Penry Williams, *The Later Tudors*, 1995.

Source G

The English fleet at this time was small in comparison with their enemies, and all people in England were thrown into terror by the report of the strength of the Armada. The English admiral knew that the size and strength of the Spanish fleet would give them a great advantage in close action and so did not take his ships too near them.

▲ From a History of Britain written in the early 19th century.

Source H

Let tyrants fear. I have always so behaved myself that, under God, I have placed my chiefest strength and safeguard in the loyal hearts and goodwill of my subjects.

I know that I have the body of a weak and feeble woman, but I have the heart and stomach of a king, and of a king of England too, and think foul scorn that Parma, or Spain, or any Prince of Europe should dare to invade the borders of my realm.

▲ Elizabeth speaks to her assembled troops at Tilbury in August 1588. The Spanish Armada was, by this time, already sailing north on its way home.

QUESTION

1 Why did Philip decide to go to war against England? Use what you have read so far in this section to help you to give and explain as many reasons for this as you can find.

Source I

▲ This shows the English fireship attack on the Spanish fleet off Calais. It was painted by the Dutch artist Hendrik Corneliz Vroom.

The Armada was first sighted by an English ship off the Lizard, in Cornwall, on 19 July. The Spanish fleet sailed slowly up the Channel, close to the English coastline and followed by the English Admiral, Lord Howard of Effingham, Sir Francis Drake and a fleet of about 90 ships. Medina Sidonia shortly discovered that Parma and his army would not be ready to meet him at the coast until a week later than expected. While the Spanish fleet waited in the channel the English sent across fireships. None of these hit a Spanish ship but they were enough for the Spanish to take up anchor and set off in disorder. The south-westerly wind prevented them from returning to pick up Parma's army. The Spanish fleet was bombarded by the short-range English guns. On 3 August Medina Sidonia ordered the fleet to return to Spain. The wind and the English fleet forced the Spanish to sail north and then north-west round the far north coast of Scotland and then south via the west coast of Ireland. Irish rocks destroyed more ships than the English guns. When the Armada reached Spain it had lost 51 ships. The English lost none.

QUESTIONS

1 Read Sources F and G. Both of these sources compare the English and Spanish fleets.
   a What are the differences between the sources?
   b Can you suggest any reasons for these differences?

2 Elizabeth's speech (Source H), has often been given as an example of her strength as Queen. How reliable is this source as evidence of this strength?

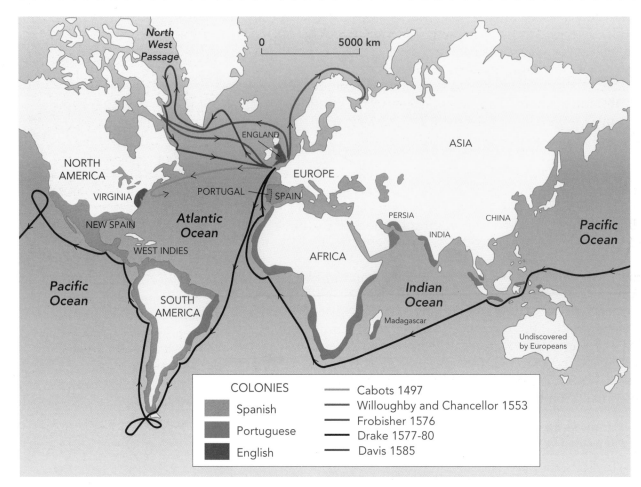

COLONIES

- Spanish
- Portuguese
- English

— Cabots 1497
— Willoughby and Chancellor 1553
— Frobisher 1576
— Drake 1577-80
— Davis 1585

▲ This map shows voyages of exploration made by English seamen between 1553 and 1603.

In 1497 during the reign of Henry VII, two Venetian merchants working in Bristol, John Cabot and his son Sebastian, discovered the territories in North America that came to be called Newfoundland and Nova Scotia. After this English exploration of the world did not begin seriously again until the reign of Mary I. Meanwhile the lead had been taken in exploration and discovery by Spain and Portugal. They established **colonies** in Asia, Central and South America and Africa. In 1553, however, Sir Hugh Willoughby and Richard Chancellor set out to find a north eastern sea trading route to India and the east. Willoughby died at sea. Chancellor did not find a north-east passage but did reach Moscow where the ruler Ivan IV welcomed him, and a year after Chancellor reached home again the Muscovy Company was founded to trade between England and Russia.

Source A

▲ Drake's ship, the *Pelican*. It was later renamed the *Golden Hind*.

In 1577 Francis Drake set off westwards on a voyage to try to found a colony in South America and to establish trading connections with China. As you read earlier in this chapter Drake also wanted to take revenge on the Spanish treatment of English ships and seamen at San Juan de Ulua. He failed to set up a colony in South America though his contact with China enabled English merchants to start trading there. He also took a substantial amount of gold and silver from Spanish ships. His most important achievement was, however, that he was the first Englishman to sail round the world.

Between 1576 and 1578 Martin Frobisher led three expeditions to try to find a route north west over what is now Canada, to India and the east. He failed, as did John Davis in 1585. They did, however, make an important contribution to knowledge of the north east of the North American continent.

Elizabeth wanted to establish an English colony in North America. She nearly succeeded. Sir Walter Raleigh organised a crossing of the Atlantic in 1585, under Sir Richard Grenville. His men settled on Roanoke Island, in what is now the US State of Virginia, but after five years of trying to support settlers on the island Elizabeth forbade any more ships to go there: it was too expensive and too difficult. Virginia was eventually settled in 1607, in James I's reign.

Elizabeth had more success in sending ships to set up trade in the Mediterranean and the East Indies. In 1581 Elizabeth gave the Turkey Company, later known as the **Levant Company**, the sole right to trade with the ports of the Turkish Empire. They sold English cloth in return for raw silk and currants. In 1600 the **East India Company** was set up to take control of trade with the Indies.

Source **B**

Throughout the evening and the whole of the night the *Revenge*, bombarded from every side, fought off her attackers until her powder had run out and forty of her crew of one hundred were dead. Grenville, mortally wounded, ordered the ship to be scuttled but his crew refused, and the Spaniards accepted an honourable surrender. The gallant fight of the *Revenge* became immortal, but the expedition was, for all that, a failure.

▲ The historian Penry Williams describes the last stand of the *Revenge* against the Spaniards in 1591 after an English raid on Spanish treasure ships.

Source **C**

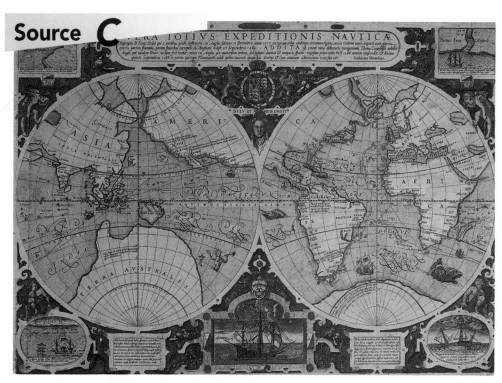

▶ This map was made and published in London in about 1590. It shows Drake's voyage around the world, 1577-1580 as well as a later voyage made by Thomas Cavendish in 1586-88.

During Elizabeth's reign English sea power increased considerably. There were more ships, which were bigger in size and designed well enough to cope with the winds and the waves of long sea voyages. By 1603, however, England still had a long way to go to catch up with the achievements of Spain and Portugal in establishing and supporting colonies in different parts of the known world. Elizabeth had, however, laid the foundations for England to establish the British Empire.

QUESTION

What were the most important achievements of English seamen in their voyages into the wider world beyond Europe?

5.5 Exercise

Source 1

▶ The people in this painting are Philip II, the Duke of Alençon, the Duke of Alva, William of Orange and Elizabeth I. The cow represents the Spanish Netherlands.

1 Make short notes about the links, during the first few years of Elizabeth's reign, between:
 a Scotland and France;
 b England and Scotland;
 c England and France.

 d Spain and the Netherlands;
 e England and Spain;
 f England and the Netherlands.

2 Use the notes which you have made for Question 1 to help you to answer these questions:
 a Why did England and France start Elizabeth's reign at war but spend most of the rest of the reign as allies?

 b Why did England and Spain start Elizabeth's reign as allies but spend the last 18 years of the reign at war with each other?

3 Look carefully at Source 1. Study the men in the painting. One is riding the cow; one is leading it; one is milking it and one is holding the cow's tail.
 a Use your knowledge of these men to try to identify them. Explain why you have decided which is which.
 b Why is Elizabeth shown feeding the cow?
 c What is the painting saying about the situation in the Netherlands?

CHAPTER 6

REBELLION AND RESISTANCE

You read in Chapter 2 that Elizabeth was not able to do everything she thought right without some protest. In Parliament and Privy Council this protest was limited to words. There were, however, some people who were prepared to express their feelings in open, sometimes armed, rebellion. Two such events were the rebellion of the Northern Earls (1569-70) and, nearly at the end of Elizabeth's reign, the rebellion of the Earl of Essex (1601).

Elizabeth also had problems with Ireland. English attempts to rule Ireland dated back to Henry II of England (1154-1189) who had declared himself Lord of Ireland. In 1540 Elizabeth's father, Henry VIII, decided that he should be called King of Ireland. There was increasing Irish resistance to the English attempts to extend the areas under their influence in Ireland. The whole situation became more complicated in Elizabeth's reign because Catholic Spain supported the Catholic Irish when they took up arms against English rule. This was a recipe for disaster, and the Earl of Essex was one of the victims.

6.1 The rebellion of the Northern Earls

For hundreds of years the north of England had been very much in the powerful hands of the noble families whose lands lay in Northumberland, Cumberland and Westmorland. After the Catholic uprising of 1537 known as the **Pilgrimage of Grace** Henry VIII established the Council of the North to try to keep control of the north from London. He also stripped the Earl of Northumberland of his earldom and took over his lands. The Catholic Queen Mary I gave the earl back his title and his lands. When Elizabeth I came to the throne she tried to limit the powers of the earls by putting southern lords in charge of some of their lands

▶ **This map shows the northern counties where the rebel earls lived and ruled.**

No. Those that seem to take that quarrel in other countries, are thought to be rebels. I will never blot my family which has been this long preserved without staining.

▲ The Earl of Westmorland gave this answer to his Catholic officers when they urged him to rebel for the sake of religion.

Source **B**

Question: What was the intent and meaning of the rebellion?
Answer: Our first object was the reformation of religion and the preservation of the person of the Queen of Scots, as next heir, failing issue of Her Majesty, which causes I believed were greatly favoured by most of the noblemen of the realm.

▲ The Earl of Northumberland explains the reasons for the rebellion when he is officially questioned.

QUESTIONS

1 Why did Leicester and some other nobles support the idea of marriage between Norfolk and Mary Queen of Scots?

2 Why was the rebellion of the Northern Earls so dangerous to Elizabeth?

and making the Earl of Sussex president of the Council. A further complication was that the Earl of Westmorland was married to the sister of Thomas Howard, Duke of Norfolk. Norfolk was a member of the Privy Council and probably a Catholic (though he denied it at his death). Some of Elizabeth's councillors thought that Norfolk should marry Mary Queen of Scots, the main Catholic heir to the English throne (see Chapter 1 and also page 61).

Norfolk was thought to be Catholic enough to satisfy Mary's religious beliefs. He had also accepted Elizabeth's religious settlement (see Chapter 4). Other English nobles, including Leicester, the Queen's favourite at this time, resented Cecil's influence in the Privy Council. They thought that if Norfolk had greater importance he could help to limit Cecil's power. Cecil was very much against the marriage, as was Elizabeth. Eventually support for the marriage dropped away. At the same time the northern earls and their Catholic followers were plotting to force Elizabeth to recognise Mary as her successor. Before long Norfolk was put in the Tower.

The Earls of Northumberland and Westmorland began to gather forces together to protect themselves. Neither man, apparently, wanted to rebel against the Queen. But when Elizabeth ordered both of them to Court to explain their actions, real trouble began. Lady Westmorland (Norfolk's sister) urged rebellion. Her husband refused and protested his loyalty to the Queen. His wife won the argument. In early November, 1569, Northumberland and Westmorland rode to Durham. They and their men destroyed the English Bible and the Protestant communion table in the cathedral. They gave orders that a Catholic mass should be celebrated.

A force of about 4,000 foot soldiers and 1,800 horsemen marched south to try to arrange for Mary Queen of Scots (who was imprisoned in Sheffield castle at the time) to be married to a Catholic and recognised as heir to the English throne. They got no further than Selby, just south of York. The Earl of Sussex was sent north to crush the rebels and chased them over the Scottish border. Those who were caught were punished severely. About 600 men were executed, though the rebel leaders escaped. The Earl of Northumberland, however, who had fled to Scotland, was handed over to the English government in 1572. He was executed and his family was forbidden to live in the north. The Earl of Westmorland's lands were taken over by the crown.

6.2 The rebellion of the Earl of Essex

Robert Devereux was born in 1566. He became Earl of Essex in 1573 on the death of his father, Walter. Walter Devereux had helped to put down the northern rebels in 1569. He also served the Queen as Earl Marshal of Ireland. The Earl of Leicester married Walter's widow, Lettice, in 1578. He then became step-father to the young Earl of Essex. Leicester introduced Essex into the Court in 1587 when Essex was 21 and Elizabeth was 54. The young man soon gained the Queen's favour and she made him Master of the Horse. Essex hoped for more. Leicester died in 1588, and Elizabeth's close friend and adviser William Cecil, Lord Burghley, was crippled with the disease known as gout and getting old. His son, Robert Cecil, an intelligent, ambitious man, was a Privy Councillor. He was, however, small and hunchbacked, and the Queen, always able to appreciate an attractive man, cannot have failed to contrast him with the tall, good-looking Earl of Essex.

Essex, like others before him, was very jealous of the influence which the Cecils had in Court, but he made the most of being Elizabeth's latest favourite. She rode and hunted with him and played cards with him in her chamber until the early hours. In 1595 she made him a Privy Councillor.

The attack on Cadiz

In 1596 Essex had his first chance to gain glory for himself. In 1595 four Spanish ships had sailed over to Cornwall. The Spaniards burned Penzance, and invaded the tiny villages of Newlyn and Mousehole (pronounced 'Mowzle'). Essex suggested to the Queen that he should take a fleet over to Cadiz, in Spain, where he would establish an English garrison. She was doubtful about the wisdom of this. In 1588 England had defeated the Spanish Armada and in the years following there was an uneasy relationship between the two countries. Philip II of Spain hoped to get his own back on England but neither he nor Elizabeth wanted full-scale war, mainly because they could not afford it. The Cecils and their supporters supported Elizabeth's view; other Privy Councillors, including Essex, urged war.

▲ Robert Devereux, Earl of Essex. This portrait is thought to have been painted in 1596 by Marcus Gheeraerts the younger.

Source **B**

He told me with his own mouth that he looked to be Master of the Horse within these ten days. At night, my Lord of Essex is at cards, or one game or another with her, that he cometh not to his own lodgings till birds sing in the morning.

▲ Anthony Bagot, Essex' servant, describes his master's relationship with Elizabeth soon after he was introduced into the Court.

In April 1596 the Spanish attacked and took the French town of Calais, just across the English Channel. Elizabeth now agreed that Essex should attack the Spanish port of Cadiz. In June Essex set out with soldiers and 150 ships commanded by Lord Howard of Effingham. On the arrival of the English fleet in Cadiz the Spanish burned their own fleet rather than let it be taken. Essex and his men attacked the town, but not until he had let all the women and children seek safety, with as many belongings as they could take with them.

Quarrel with the Queen

Essex returned to England a hero. In 1597 Elizabeth made him Earl Marshal of England, an important and influential post, but he still wanted more. He suggested sending a bigger force against Spain but Robert Cecil and his father, now very ill, opposed this. In the summer of 1598 Essex became involved in an argument with the Queen because she would not appoint one of his friends, Sir George Carew, as her Lord Deputy in Ireland. He angrily turned his back on her, whereupon she boxed his ears. He almost drew his sword, but was restrained by one of the courtiers. He shouted that he would not have put up with such an insult even from her father, and stormed out of the room.

Elizabeth put him under arrest in his own house. He could not accept that he was in the wrong. In a letter to Elizabeth he referred to 'the intolerable wrong that you have done both me and yourself' which had 'not only broken all laws of affection, but had been done against the honour of your sex.' The Queen took no further action against him, probably because she was upset and distracted by the illness of Lord Burghley. Burghley died in August, 1598.

Essex in Ireland

In January 1599 Elizabeth made Essex Lord Lieutenant of Ireland, with the express intent that he should deal with the unruly Irish. Elizabeth, like previous Tudor monarchs, was trying to gain greater control of Ireland. This was partly because of a desire to expand English power but also because the Irish could – and often did – offer help and support to England's enemies (see Chapter 5). Essex sailed for Ireland in March 1599 with 16,000 foot soldiers and 1,000 horsemen.

Essex angered Elizabeth almost as soon as he landed by appointing one of his friends, the Earl of Southampton, as cavalry commander. Elizabeth did not approve of Southampton and had forbidden Essex to appoint him to any position. He also knighted about eighty men during the time he was in Ireland, also against the Queen's wishes. Worst of all, he failed to crush the Earl of Tyrone, the Irish leader. He

Source C

I owe her Majesty the duty of an Earl and of Lord Marshal of England. I have been content to do her Majesty the service of a clerk, but I can never serve her as a villein or a slave. Cannot Princes err? Cannot subjects receive wrong?

▲ The Earl of Essex writes to Elizabeth after the ear-boxing episode.

Source D

If we had intended that Ireland, after all the problems there, should have been abandoned, we certainly would not have sent someone of your rank over there.

▲ Elizabeth wrote this in a letter to Essex just before Essex came back to England against her wishes.

Source E

What madness is it for a General to lead royal forces against naked rogues in woods and bogs, whom hounds can scarcely follow, and much less men.

▲ Official comment from state documents on Essex's tactics in Ireland in 1599.

agreed a truce with him, again against the Queen's will. This gave Tyrone time to ask for Spanish support (see page 77).

Elizabeth sent a letter to Essex forbidding him to leave his post in Ireland. He did not receive this, for he rushed home in September 1599 to celebrate his truce with Tyrone. Arriving dirty and dishevelled from his journey he burst into the Queen's bed-chamber and caught her just out of bed and without her red wig. By the afternoon it was clear that Elizabeth did not share Essex's joy in his truce. Instead she ordered that he should answer to the Privy Council for his behaviour in Ireland. He was placed under house arrest.

In June 1600 there was a full enquiry into his actions and he was charged with 'misgovernance' in Ireland and deserting his post. He was stripped of all his posts and forbidden to attend Court. He also lost the right to collect the duties paid on all sweet wines imported into the country. This made him almost bankrupt. Robert Cecil, whom the Queen had made principal secretary in 1596, was given the Mastership of the Court of Wards in May 1599. Essex had badly wanted this post, which gave the holder the guardianship of the lands of all nobles who inherited estates before they came of age. It brought with it a vast income. Essex felt betrayed and let down by the Queen.

The rebellion

In February 1601 Essex drew up a plan for seizing the Court, the City of London and the Tower. He sent this to some of his supporters who discussed what they should do. The plans leaked out and Essex received a visit from four Privy Councillors, including his uncle, Sir William Knollys, and the Lord Chief Justice. He was ordered to Court. He refused, took them hostage and set out with an armed band to seek support in London. He failed. Finding his way to the Royal Court, his next goal, blocked by troops he returned to Essex House, only to find that his prisoners had been released. Lord Howard of Effingham, the man with whom Essex had sailed on his victorious expedition to Cadiz, was sent to bring him to Court. Essex surrendered, after burning all his papers. He was tried and executed for treason on 25 February 1601. The Queen's fondness for Essex could not overcome her belief that no-one should rebel against a lawful monarch.

Source F

Essex did not get the support he expected, from the nobility or from London. He was an even worse conspirator than he was a general, and he paid with his life. But it was a dramatic illustration of the growing lack of support for the Queen by the aristocracy that so many had dabbled in treason – so many, indeed, that the Queen dared not punish them.

The Earls of Rutland and Southampton and Lords Mounteagle and Sandys were deeply involved; the Earls of Bedford and Sussex and Lord Cromwell were implicated. Lord Mountjoy had contemplated using his Irish army to support Essex, and we do not know what other discontented nobles might have done if Essex had been less clumsy.

▲ The historian Christopher Haigh, writing in 1996, comments on Essex's rebellion.

QUESTIONS

1 Make a list under two headings:
   a Essex's successes
   b Essex's failures.

   If one list is longer than the other, can you draw any conclusions from this?

2 a In what ways does Source F criticise Essex?
   b In what ways does Source F support Essex?
   c Who, in the end, does Haigh blame for the fall of the Earl of Essex?

3 Why, when Elizabeth was so fond of Essex, did she agree to his execution?

◀ **This map shows the provinces of Ireland and the clan chiefs who ruled there in Elizabeth's reign.**

Earlier in this chapter you read a brief introduction to the relationship between England and Ireland. You also read about the adventures and disasters of the Earl of Essex. Why did Elizabeth have such problems with Ireland?

William Camden (Source B) uses the word 'rebellion' to describe the Irish reaction to English rule. People who rise up against those who rule them are called rebels. Camden's use of the word 'rebellion' assumes that Ireland was part of England, that the English had the right to rule over the Irish people and to expect their loyalty (or at least peace and quiet). Source A helps to explain what the English felt about the Irish. The Irish people resented the English takeover of parts of their country. They had remained Catholic and were happy to support Spain against England, just as Spain was prepared to support the Irish when they rose up against English rule. This situation created a huge threat to English security: a country just over the sea to the west of England and Wales that was willing to let foreign forces use its harbours to invade England and supply fighting men.

Source A

Thomas, Earl of Sussex, who had been in the Reign of Queen Mary Lord Deputy of Ireland, was sent back again into Ireland, with instructions that he should above all things beware, lest the Irish (being an uncivilised people) should by the cunning practices of the French be led to rebellion on account of religion.

▲ **William Camden, writing shortly after Elizabeth's death, shows what the English thought of the Irish at the time that Sussex was sent to be Lord Deputy in 1559.**

The Irish attitude is also understandable. The English occupation of the 'Pale' around Dublin had taken place in the 12th century, and English settlers had gone to Ireland to try to extend English influence over the whole country. These families had, by Elizabeth's reign, became as Irish as the Irish, and some were fiercely opposed to English attempts to rule the whole of Ireland. Some clan chiefs (though not always all members of their families) supported the English. Thomas, Earl of Ormond was unswervingly loyal to Elizabeth in his part of Munster. The FitzGeralds of Desmond, however, were one of the greatest threats to English rule in the south of Ireland, as were the O'Neills of Tyrone in the North.

The Tyrone Rebellion

The English managed to control the situation until 1594, when Hugh O'Neill, Earl of Tyrone, led an uprising in Ulster. In 1598 he defeated an English army and seemed to be supreme in Ireland. It was at this point that Essex was sent to Ireland, in 1599. The truce which he agreed gave Tyrone time to wait for Spanish help. It was fortunate for Elizabeth that the next man to be sent to Ireland, Charles Blount, Lord Mountjoy, was able to beat Tyrone back into his own Ulster lands and restore order in the English Pale. Fighting lasted, on and off – with Spanish help – until Tyrone surrendered in March 1603, a few days after Elizabeth's death.

Source C

The ordinary state of Ireland was war – cattle raids, the burning of the countryside, the murder of its people. Outside the Pale there was hardly ever anything like peace and order. The Protestant religion had no hold at all, but neither did Catholicism.

The Elizabethan break with Rome meant that action was necessary. Ireland now became a possible landing-place for hostile forces. At the beginning of Elizabeth's reign Ireland was virtually ungoverned and un-Christian. By the end it was firmly under English control and Catholic.

▲ Geoffrey Elton summarises the situation in Ireland, *England under the Tudors*, 1955.

Source B

Neither at this time was Ireland free from rebellions. For the Earl of Ormond's brothers attacked their neighbours in Munster and joined with the Pope and the Spaniard to maintain their religion and to get Queen Elizabeth out of her Kingdom of Ireland.

▲ William Camden describes the situation in Ireland in 1569.

Source D

Our only hope of re-establishing the Catholic religion rests on your assistance. We again beg you to send us 2–3,000 soldiers, with money and arms. With such aid we hope to restore the Church, and secure you a kingdom.

▲ From a letter by Tyrone and O'Donnell to Philip II in September 1595.

6.4 Exercise

1 Read Sources A, B, C and D.

   a Does Source C support Sources A, B and D in suggesting that the main reason for the problems between England and Ireland was their difference in religion?

   b What other reasons can you find for the English desire to rule Ireland?

2 Read pages 71-7.
   Find as many reasons as you can to explain why

   a the northern earls rebelled against Elizabeth.
   b the Earl of Essex rebelled against Elizabeth.
   c the Irish people resisted English rule in Ireland.

3 What *different reasons* did people have for challenging Elizabeth's decisions or policies?

CHAPTER 7

THE ELIZABETHANS AT LEISURE

Has the game of football changed since Philip Stubbes wrote his description in 1583 (Source A)? Professional football matches are now played according to rules which try to prevent fighting and foul play, though this does not stop players from fighting each other when things go wrong. There are, also, some villages in many parts of Britain where games of football are played which would have been recognised by people who lived in Elizabeth's time. These have been played for many centuries and players often end up with bloody noses or even broken limbs.

The Elizabethans enjoyed a variety of sports and pastimes, many of them out-of-doors. There were only candles or oil-lamps to provide indoor light when the sun went down so it was difficult to play indoor games.

Time for sports and pastimes was very limited for ordinary people. They usually worked for six days of the week. On Sundays and other holidays men were supposed to practice archery in case they were needed as soldiers in wartime. Clearly, not everyone obeyed this ancient law, or the number of sports and other pastimes in which working people took part would not have been as great as it was. The rich and the poor enjoyed different activities. The rich had more time as well as more money to spend and so were able to take part in a wider range of sports and pastimes.

During Elizabeth's reign both rich and poor people, especially those living in London, began to spend more time going to the theatre. They watched plays written by Ben Johnson, Christopher Marlowe and William Shakespeare in theatres like the Swan and the Globe. Not everyone, however, approved of going to the theatre. Puritans would have agreed with the description of a theatre in 1580, as 'the chapel of Satan' (see Source B).

Source A

As concerning football playing, I protest to you it may rather be called a friendly kind of fight, than a recreation; a bloody and murdering practice than a friendly sport or pastime.
For does not everyone lie in wait for his opponent, seeking to overthrow him and throw him on his nose on hard stones, in a ditch or wherever?
He does not care as long as he gets him down. So that by this means, sometimes their necks are broken, sometimes their backs, sometimes their legs, sometimes their noses gush out with blood.

▲ A description of football, as played in the 16th century, written by Philip Stubbes in 1583. Stubbes was a Puritan and disapproved of people spending their leisure time playing games such as this.

Source B

Will not a filthy play, with the blast of a trumpet, sooner call there a thousand (people) than an hour's tolling of a church bell will bring a hundred to the sermon?

▲ John Stockwood, a Puritan, expressed his fears about the appeal of theatres in a sermon preached outside in London in 1578.

Source C

Common bowling alleys eat up the money of many idle citizens whose shops are so far from making up for their play that their wives and children cry out for bread, and go to bed without supper often in the year.

▲ From a book written by Stephen Gosson in 1579. He was a Church of England clergyman who wrote plays and poems.

Source D

In May men, women and children go into the woods and bring home their May-pole (this stinking idol, rather). It is covered all over with flowers and herbs, bound around with strings from the top to the bottom, and sometimes painted with variable colours. Everyone follows it with great devotion. They then fall to banquet and feast and to leap and dance about it.

▲ Written in 1583 by Philip Stubbes, the Puritan.

Source E

In the city of London cock-fights are held throughout most of the year. I saw the place, which is built like a theatre. In the centre on the floor stands a circular table covered with straw with ledges round it, where cocks are teased and encouraged to fly at one another.

Those with bets as to which cock will win sit closest around the circular table, but those only watching sit around higher up, watching with pleasure the fierce and angry fight between the cocks, as these wound each other to death with their beaks.

▲ Thomas Platter, a German traveller in England, wrote this in 1599.

The best way of finding out about the sports and pastimes enjoyed by rich and poor in Elizabeth's England is to read what people wrote and to look at drawings made at the time. The sources on the next few pages will help you to do this.

People at play in the towns and the villages

Source F

▲ A 17th century woodcut showing bull and bear-baiting.

Source G

The baiting of a bear, besides that it is a filthy, stinking and loathsome game, is this not a dangerous exercise, wherein a man is in danger of his life every minute of an hour? What Christian heart can take pleasure to see one poor beast to rent, tear and kill another, and all for his foolish pleasure? Although they be bloody beasts to mankind, yet we are not to abuse them, for the sake of God who made them, and whose creatures they are.

▲ Philip Stubbes on bear-baiting, 1583.

Source **H**

When the great fen or moor on the north side of the city of London is frozen, many young men play upon the ice, some striding as wide as they may, do slide swiftly. Others make themselves seats of ice as great as millstones: one sits down, many hand-in-hand do draw him, and one slipping suddenly, all fall together. Some tie bones to their feet and under their heels and shoving themselves by a little staff do slide as swiftly as a bird flies in the air, or an arrow out of a crossbow.

▲ John Stow wrote this in his 'Survey of London', published in 1598.

Source **I**

The exercise of running at the Quintain was practised by the youthful citizens, as well in summer as in winter, especially at Christmas. He that hits not the broad end of the Quintain with his tilt was laughed at by all men; and he that hit it full, if he rode not faster after that, had a sound blow in the neck, with a bag full of sand hanging on the other end.

▲ From John Stow's 'Survey of London', published in 1598. A quintain was a post fixed in the ground with a revolving crossbar. This had a shield hanging from one end, and a heavy bag of sand from the other. The idea was to run and hit the shield with a long spear (tilt) and move quickly before the sand bag swung round and hit the tilter.

The rich at play

Source **J**

Monday was hot. Therefore her highness Queen Elizabeth I kept in till five o'clock in the evening. Then she rode forth into the chase to hunt the deer. Chased by the hounds it ran towards the water. The stately carriage of the deer's head in swimming, the baying of the hounds, then the swiftness of the deer running, the galloping of horses, the blasting of horns, the halloing and shouts of the huntsmen, with the excellent echoes from the woods and waters in valleys resounding made a delightful pastime for all the senses. There can be nothing comparable to this.

◀ From a letter written by Robert Laneham in 1575 describing the hunt at Kenilworth Castle.

▼ A woodcut made in 1577 showing jousting. This was similar to tilting at the quintain (Source I) but jousting was only for the nobles, being carried out on horse-back, in full armour.

Source **K**

Source L

▲ Tennis, as played in the late 16th century.

Source M

▲ A woodcut from George Turbervile's 'Book of Falconrie', 1575.

Source N

Bowls was played by gentlemen, priests and university fellows. After Archbishop Cranmer had been kept for many months in the common jail in Oxford he was transferred to the custody of the Dean of the college of Christ Church. He was kindly treated and allowed to play bowls on the village green.

There is no reason to doubt the truth of the story that Drake was playing bowls on Plymouth Hoe when he was told that the Armada had been sighted off the Lizard, and famously said that there was time enough to finish the game.

He was quite right, for it was not until eight hours later that the tide was right for the English ships to be rowed out. The story was first recorded in writing in the 18th century, but there is reference in a publication of 1624 to the fact that English captains were playing bowls when the Armada was sighted. As this was only 36 years later, there were many people still alive who remembered 1588 and the story may have been told by someone who was present.

▲ From *The Tudor Age*, by Jasper Ridley, 1988.

QUESTIONS

1 a Make a list of the different sports and pastimes which are shown in Sources A-M.
   b Which of these do you think were enjoyed by the rich?
   c Which of these do you think were enjoyed by the poor?
   d Think of as many reasons as you can to explain why rich and poor enjoyed different leisure activities.

2 Which of the activities listed here are still enjoyed today? Try to suggest reasons
   a why have some survived
   b why some have disappeared.

At the beginning of the 16th century many plays performed to the public were based on religious themes. These are sometimes called 'morality plays' and showed good and bad conduct. Others, called 'miracle plays' showed scenes from the Bible. The main exception to this were the plays put on by wandering groups of actors, known as 'strolling players'. The plays acted by the players were often far from religious and the authorities tried to ban them. During the 16th century, however, England was influenced by the European movement known as the 'Renaissance'. This led to an enormous flowering of music, art and literature. Unlike in previous centuries, composers, artists and writers did not base everything on religious themes and ideas. English playwrights began to write comedies and tragedies. Tragedies were often based on well-known historical events. Richard III was a favourite subject: eight plays are known to have been written about him. Some plays were about more recent events. For example, 'The King of Scots' was about the murder in 1567 of Lord Darnley, Mary Queen of Scots' husband. It was first performed shortly after his death.

It was not, however, until the very last years of Elizabeth's reign that playwrights like Ben Jonson, Christopher Marlowe and William Shakespeare began to write the plays for which they are now famous. This was mainly because it had been difficult to get a company of actors together to put on a play. In 1572 the Act of Parliament 'for the punishment of vagabonds and the relief of the poor' was passed. This ordered the punishment of actors unless they were employed by noblemen. Wandering actors or strolling players were unpopular with the

Source A

▲ This is the title-page of the script of the morality play *Everyman*. It was published in about 1509. The words read:
'Here begynneth a treatyse how the hye father of heven sendeth dethe to somon every creature to come and gyve a counte of theyr lyves in this worlde and is in maner of a morall playe'.

Source B

▶ Portrait of Christopher Marlowe.

Plays and Playwrights

Christopher Marlowe was born in 1564 in Canterbury. He went to Cambridge University and then lived in London. His first play was *Tamburlaine*, produced in 1587. This was based (very loosely) on the life of an Asian ruler, Timur i Leng. He wrote five more plays before he was killed in a fight in London in 1593 at the age of 49.

William Shakespeare was born in 1564 in Stratford-upon-Avon, where he went to school. He lived and worked in London from about 1585, but returned to Stratford a few years before his death in 1616. His first play, *The Contention betwixt the Two Noble Houses of York and Lancaster* was produced in 1592. This is now known as *Henry VI, Parts II and III*. Though most of his plays were written and performed after Elizabeth's death, some of his most famous plays, like *A Midsummer Night's Dream*, *Romeo and Juliet*, *The Merchant of Venice*, *Julius Caesar* and *Hamlet* were written and performed between 1592 and 1603.

Ben Jonson was born in 1572 in London, where he went to Westminster School. Most of his plays were written and produced after Elizabeth's death. However, his comedy *Every Man in his Humour* was put on at the Globe Theatre in 1598. Shakespeare took a leading role as an actor in its first performances. The play was about the disagreements between those people who smoked tobacco and those who didn't. Tobacco was only introduced into England in 1585 when Sir Francis Drake brought some back from the West Indies. It was smoked in clay pipes: many people disapproved of it but many people enjoyed it. Ben Jonson died in 1637 and is buried in Westminster Abbey.

authorities because of the type of plays which they performed. It was often difficult to tell the difference between some strolling players and wandering beggars. It was only because noblemen supported companies of actors that plays by Jonson, Marlowe and Shakespeare could be performed in public.

The Earl of Leicester, in 1574, was the first nobleman to pay a company of actors to put on plays for the people of London. They used the courtyard of the Bull Inn in Bishopsgate. To begin with, before London theatres like the Globe, the Swan and the Rose were built, all plays were performed in the courtyards of inns. Elizabeth enjoyed watching plays, including Shakespeare's. This certainly helped playwrights to grow in importance so that they and their actors were no longer regarded as vagabonds.

Source D

▲ This portrait of William Shakespeare appeared on the title page of a book of his plays published in 1623 after his death.

Source C

I marvel what pleasure they have in taking this tobacco; it's good for nothing but to choke a man, and fill him full of smoke and embers. There were four died out of one house last week with taking of it, and two more yesternight. One of them, they say, will never escape it; he got rid of a bushel of soot yesterday, upward and downward.

◀ A character in Jonson's play *Every Man in his Humour* gives his opinion about smoking tobacco.

Actors

Some actors became famous and well respected. Richard Burbage was one of the most famous actors of the late 16th and early 17th centuries. Shakespeare wrote *Othello*, *King Lear* and *Hamlet* with Burbage in mind for the main parts. Shakespeare himself began his career as an actor. He was a member of the Lord Chamberlain's Company when he acted in Ben Johnson's comedy Every man in His Humour in 1598. He received a royal licence for his own company in 1603, early in the reign of Elizabeth's successor, James I.

Until the 1660s women did not act in plays. Women's parts were played by young boys. Shakespeare used this to good effect in a number of his plays in which women, played by boys, pretended to be young men. For example, in *As You Like It* Rosalind pretends to be Orlando, a young man. In *The Merchant of Venice* Portia and her friend Nerissa dress as young men to confuse their husbands.

The Theatres

Watching plays became more and more popular with people of all classes and ages. This led to the need to build theatres where these plays could be staged, instead of using the courtyards of inns. In 1576, James Burbage organised the building of a theatre which would only be used for performing plays. His theatre, called simply 'The Theatre' was successful, and inspired him to open another theatre in 1577, called 'The Curtain'. The popularity of stage plays in the years after this led to the building of the Rose, the Swan and the Globe Theatres in London between 1587 and 1598.

The Globe Theatre has been recently reconstructed (see Source F). This has given us a very clear idea of what a theatre looked like in Elizabeth's time. The reconstruction was based on the work of archaeologists and drawings made at the time the Globe was originally built.

Elizabethan theatres were different from modern-day theatres. To begin with, there was a large, central, open space known as the 'yard' which was open to

Source E

▲ The Swan Theatre.

the sky. The numbers of people who could watch a play were similar to today. The Globe, for example, could hold 800 people in its yard and 2,000 in its galleries.

Plays had to be performed in daylight, usually in the afternoon. There would be no performance if the weather was very bad. The stage, which did have a roof, projected into the yard. All round the yard were roofed galleries of tiered seats. The yard, which was open to rain and wind, was where ordinary people stood to watch the play. These were known as the 'groundlings'. The galleries, which were covered, were where better-off people sat.

Another difference between Elizabethan theatres and those built later is that there were no curtains to separate the stage and its actors from the audience. In most theatres today the different scenes of a play are separated by curtains being drawn between the stage and the audience. Actors are able to change clothes and stage hands to change the scenery to show a change in time or place. In Elizabeth's time the words and timing of the play had to give the actors time to go off-stage and change clothes, and in fact this is usually the way Shakespeare is produced today.

QUESTIONS

1 Find out and write down the meaning of these terms; *morality plays, strolling players, the Renaissance.*

2 Why was it not until so late in Elizabeth's reign that companies of actors could safely put on plays for the public to watch?

3 Make two columns, headed 'Theatres today' and '16th century theatres'. Make lists, under these headings, of the main differences between them. Use Sources E and F, as well as the text, to help you.

4 Why do you think people today have been prepared to spend a great deal of time and money on reconstructing the Globe theatre?

Source E

▲ **This photograph shows the reconstructed Globe Theatre. It was opened for public performances in 1997.**

Many enjoyed the theatre...

Many people of all classes enjoyed going to the theatre. Thomas White's observation that people flocked to the theatre (Source A) is backed up by research carried out by the historian Andrew Gurr. He has estimated that 15,000 people visited the theatre in London each week in 1595. This was when there were only two theatres open. Numbers rose to 25,000 a week by 1620 when there were six theatres. Elizabeth enjoyed watching plays. She used to invite companies of actors to perform at Court. In February 1579 she so much enjoyed a play put on by the Lord Chamberlain's players that she gave them a large reward.

...Some disapproved of the theatre

As Source B shows, the theatre was not popular with everyone. Puritans disapproved of people spending time watching plays which they thought did them no good. The authorities of the City of London believed that theatres attracted thieves and ruffians. In fact, the Theatre, the Curtain, the Globe, the Rose and the Swan were all built outside the City of London to avoid the authorities clamping down on the performances. Philip Stubbes sums up Puritan feelings about plays in Source E. Puritans were also worried that people would rather watch a play which would teach them bad habits than go to church to learn how to follow God's ways.

Source A

Look but upon the common plays in London and see the multitude that flock to them and follow them!

▲ Thomas White, a Puritan, said this during a sermon preached in London in November 1577.

Source B

Whosoever shall visit the chapel of Satan, I mean the theatre, shall find there no lack of young ruffians.

▲ A Puritan gives his view of the theatre in 1580.

Source C

Our late Queen Elizabeth of Blessed Memory, how well she approved of the performances in the theatre, being as she termed them 'harmless spenders of time.'

▲ Richard Brathwait describes Elizabeth's attitude towards the theatre in a book written in 1641.

Source D

A PLEASANT Conceited Comedie CALLED, Loues labors loft.

As it vvas prefented before her Highnes this laft Chriftmas.

Newly corrected and augmented By *W. Shakeſpere.*

Imprinted at London by *W.W.* for *Cutbert Burby* 1598.

▶ The title page of the first edition of Shakespeare's *Love's Labours Lost* (1598), shows that the Queen has seen the play.

The authorities had good reason to stop people from going to the theatre. The plays encouraged young apprentices to skip work. Crowds of people encouraged pickpockets and the spread of fatal diseases like the plague and smallpox. Theatres were, in fact, closed if the death rate from the plague was high at any time. In relation to this Source F brings together quite neatly the fears of Puritans and the fears of city and town authorities.

Source E

Do they not encourage whoredom and uncleanness? For proof of this look at the daily flocking and running to Theatres and Curtains to see plays where such bawdy speeches, such laughing, such kissing, such winking and glancing of wanton eyes and the like is used.

▲ Philip Stubbes explains in 1583 why he disapproves of theatres.

Source F

Plays are banished for a time out of London, lest those going to see them should get the plague. Would to God these common plays were got rid of altogether as learning places of ungodliness, and their theatres pulled down as no better than bawdy-houses.

▲ William Harrison, an historian and Church of England clergyman, wrote this shortly before he died in 1593.

Source G

Theatres are the regular places for vagabonds, thieves, contrivers of treason and other idle and dangerous persons to meet together to the great displeasure of Almighty God and the hurt and annoyance of her Majesty's people. This cannot be prevented by the governors of the City of London for they are out of the city's jurisdiction.
They maintain idleness in such persons as have no job, and draw apprentices and other servants from their ordinary work.
In the time of sickness many who have sores amuse themselves by hearing a play, whereby others are infected.

▲ The Lord Mayor and other important officials of the City of London wrote this in a letter to the Privy Council in July 1597.

Source H

Your Lordships do permit the three Companies of Players publicly to exercise their plays in their usual houses, namely the Globe in Maiden Lane, the Fortune in Golding Lane and the Curtain in Holywell. This is without any interruption unless more than thirty should die weekly of the plague within the City of London. At this time we think it fit that they shall cease to play publicly until the sickness be decreased to thirty or below.

▲ The Privy Council orders that theatres shall be closed when deaths from the plague rise above 30 a week.

QUESTIONS

1 a Look carefully at the sources on these pages. How many different reasons can you find for opposition to the theatres?
  b A number of different Puritans as well as a Church of England clergyman were critical of the theatre. Does this prove that theatre-going had a bad effect on people? Explain your answer.

2 Look at Sources C and D.
How could you use Source D to support what Source C says about Elizabeth's attitude towards theatre-going?

3 Sources F and H both refer to closing theatres because of the plague. In which ways do these sources *differ* in describing the attitudes shown towards plays and theatre-going?

4 Why, despite criticisms and disapproval, was the theatre so popular and successful in Elizabeth's reign?

Source 1

On, on you noblest English!
I see you stand like greyhounds in the slips,
Straining upon the start. The game's afoot:
Follow your spirit; and upon this charge
Cry 'God for Harry! England and Saint George!

▲ From Shakespeare's *Henry V*, Act III, Scene ii

Source 2

Heaven take my soul, and England keep my bones!

▲ From Shakespeare's *King John*, Act IV, Scene iii.

Source 3

This England never did, nor never shall,
Lie at the proud foot of a conqueror.

▲ From Shakespeare's *King John*, Act V, Scene vii.

Source 4

This royal throne of kings, this sceptred isle,
This happy breed of men, this little world,
This precious stone set in the silver sea,
This blessed plot, this earth, this realm, this England.

▲ From Shakespeare's *Richard II*, Act II, Scene i.

Source 5

O noble English! that could take on
With half their forces the full pride of France,
And let another half stand laughing by,
All out of work, and cold for action.

▲ From Shakespeare's *Henry V*, Act I, Scene ii

Source 6

▲ Painting of Elizabeth and the Earl of Leicester at Kenilworth castle, attributed to Dirck Hals (1591–1656).

1 Pick out the words and phrases which Shakespeare uses in Sources 1-5 to describe his feelings about England.

2 Use what you have learned so far about Elizabeth's England to try to explain whether people watching the plays would have agreed with Shakespeare's feelings. Support your answer with examples (see Source 6) which could explain people's pride in their country, or why they might be critical of what had happened since Elizabeth came to the throne.

CHAPTER 8

'I COUNT THIS THE GLORY OF MY CROWN, THAT I HAVE REIGNED WITH YOUR LOVES.'

8.1 How successful was Elizabeth I as Queen of England?

Elizabeth I ruled England for 45 years. She lived and reigned for longer than her grandfather, Henry VII, her father Henry VIII, her brother Edward VI and her sister Mary I.

Was this long reign successful? Was England stronger at Elizabeth's death than it was when she came to the throne?

Did Elizabeth achieve her aims for England?

Before a **general election** takes place today, each political party sets out its aims and what, if elected, it would hope to achieve, in what is called a 'manifesto'. Kings and queens in times past did nothing like this. Elizabeth inherited problems from her sister, Mary, and had to do what she could to solve them. She did not set the situation out in a speech or in writing. On the day before her Coronation on 15 January 1558, she went on a procession through London, through streets lined with cheering people, to meet the Lord Mayor and other important people, and to watch **pageants** and plays performed in her honour. Her speech of thanks to the Lord Mayor expressed what she wanted to achieve in personal terms (Source A). Did she carry out her promises? To answer this, you will need to answer some more specific questions.

Was England stronger at Elizabeth's death than at her accession?

If you look back to Chapter 1 and read Source C on page 5 you will see that Armigal Waad was very critical of the state of England at Elizabeth's accession. By the end of Elizabeth's reign, however, no-one would describe England as exhausted. How could anyone say that England lacked good captains and soldiers when they remember Drake, Hawkins and Raleigh? English people were, on the whole, orderly, with a well-established system for trying to punish vagabonds and rogues and support the deserving poor.

In 1603 the French offered far less of a threat to England than they had done in 1558. Mary Queen of Scots, who had been

Source A

I thank my Lord mayor, his brethren and you all. Your request is that I should continue to be your good lady and Queen. Be ye assured that I will be as good unto you as ever any Queen was unto her people.

I do not lack will nor, I trust, shall I lack any power. And be assured that for the safety and quietness of you all I will not spare, if need be, to shed my blood. God thank you all.

▲ From a speech made by Elizabeth I in London on 14 January 1558, the eve of her Coronation.

▲ **Hardwick Hall, one of the great Elizabethan country houses.**

married to a former king of France, was dead; her Protestant son, James, was to be Elizabeth's successor, and the energies of the French king, Henry IV, were taken up with religious civil war.

You have read about all of these developments, and more. Elizabeth and her advisers had tried to sort out religious problems and differences. Rebellions had surfaced and been crushed. English poetry, music and plays flourished. The nobility built great country houses for themselves (see Source B). Unlike those built by their families before them, these were not fortified castles, for England was at peace with itself, and the Scots were increasingly unlikely to invade the northern regions.

Source **C**

At last, on 24 March 1603, sixty-nine years and six months old, the great queen died quietly, at rest with this world.

The Tudor age was over, for there were no more Tudors. Much of the Tudor success had been due to the skill of the dynasty. It was a wonderful family, and its achievements – aided by the work of many others – were impressive. A country once ravaged by internal war was now, despite external war, on the way to becoming a major power. Peace at home had brought law and order, a rising prosperity, a spreading over the globe, great things in the arts, a remarkable people.

▲ **Geoffrey Elton wrote this summary of the Tudor age in *England under the Tudors*, 1955.**

What problems did Elizabeth hand on to her successor, James I?

Elizabeth had tried to settle religion in England. Though there was, by the end of her reign, a 'Church of England' with an official prayer book there were still many people who did not want to follow this. Some Puritans wanted to break away from the Church of England so that they could worship as they wished. There were also large numbers of Catholics, especially in the north of England. They had been prepared to keep their heads down to avoid punishment, but would they feel the same when they had a new monarch, from Scotland, whom no ordinary people knew or had met?

James I inherited a far more peaceful country in 1603 than Elizabeth had done in 1558. The King of Spain, Philip III, had his own problems in Spain and the New World Colonies. The revolt in the Netherlands was not over but the King of Spain did not have enough money to try to stop England from supporting the rebels. France was involved in its own internal struggle. Both countries, therefore, were not in any position to threaten England at the moment, even if they wished to do so. Ireland alone remained an unsolved problem.

Source D

She died, having named the king of Scots, her nearest kinsman, as her successor.

Thus dies this great and glorious princess, whose vigour, intellect and generosity appear not to have been surpassed by any monarch that ever filled a throne.

As a woman, she appears to have been both unapproachable and vain, as women are likely to be. As a sovereign, her conduct, with some few exceptions, seems to have entitled her to the admiration and applause of all mankind.

▲ From a history of England written at the beginning of the 19th century.

QUESTIONS

1 How could you use Source B as evidence of the success of Elizabeth's reign?

2 Sources C and D both praise Elizabeth's successes as Queen. Source D is, however, more critical of her than Source C. What reasons can you suggest for this?

3 Make a table, as shown below, to reflect the good and bad points about Elizabeth's reign.

Government and Parliament		Religious affairs		Treatment of the poor		Foreign affairs	
Good	Bad	Good	Bad	Good	Bad	Good	Bad

Now answer these questions. Use the notes which you have made in the table as well as anything else which you can find from any of the work which you have done on Elizabethan England.

a Was England stronger at Elizabeth's death than at her succession?
b How successful was Elizabeth as Queen of England?

This book begins, as it ends, with the question 'Why do people remember Elizabeth I?' If people are asked to name some famous kings and queens in the past, many will remember Elizabeth I. Why is this? Elizabeth had her problems as queen. People at the time criticised her and historians today have made clear where she went wrong in her policies. Yet she is often remembered as 'Good Queen Bess' or 'Gloriana'. Was this because she was not only one of the very few female monarchs in our history but also reigned for a long time? Was this because her successor, James I, was nowhere near as popular as Elizabeth with the people, so that her reputation grew in the years after her death? Or was it because England flourished under her rule? Did her people love her as much as she says they do in her speech (Source 1)?

Source 1

There is no jewel, be it of never so rich a prince, which I set before this jewel: I mean your love. And although God hath raised me high, yet this I count the glory of my Crown, that I have reigned with your loves. This makes me that I do not so much rejoice that God hath made me to be a Queen, as to be a Queen over so thankful a people.

I know the title of a King is a glorious title, but assure yourself that the shining glory of princely authority hath not so dazzled the eyes of my understanding, but that I well know and remember that I am also to yield an account of my actions before God.
To be a king and wear a crown is a thing more glorious to them that see it than it is pleasant to them that bear it. For myself I was never so much taken with the glorious name and royal authority of a Queen. Rather I was delighted that God hath made me his instrument to maintain his truth and glory, and to defend this kingdom from peril, dishonour, tyranny and oppression.

There will never be a Queen sit in my seat with more enthusiasm to my country, care to my subjects than myself. Nor will there be a Queen who will sooner with willingness risk her life for your good and safety than myself. And although you have had, and may have, many princes more mighty and wise sitting in this seat, yet you never had nor shall have, any that will be more careful and loving.

▲ Adapted from a speech made by Elizabeth I to members of the House of Commons on 30 November 1602.

Source 2

There were many reasons for dissatisfaction with her rule. In refusing to name her heir, she took enormous risks for her kingdom. She kept putting off making decisions about foreign policy. She did little to strengthen her church and a great deal to weaken it. She let the Cecil group take over the court, causing opposition to this from Essex and many other of the younger nobles.

However, there is more to be said on the other side. Elizabeth had the great gift of choosing able ministers and of standing by them, giving her realm the stability that it had lacked under her father, her brother and her sister. She had a skill in public display which made her deeply admired, and, until her later years, loved by her subjects. She was perhaps the only really popular monarch between Henry V and Queen Victoria.

▲ The historian Penry Williams sums up his conclusions about Elizabeth, *The Later Tudors*, 1995.

Source 3

That Elizabeth's government was able to conduct a reasonably successful foreign policy without bankrupting the Crown was its great success. The danger lay in leaving Elizabeth's successors the myth of a glorious foreign policy that they found hard to live up to.

▲ The historian Simon Adams explains his views on Elizabeth's foreign policy, *England and the World under the Tudors*, 1996.

Source 4

After a few years of Stuart rule, the Queen's image improved. Her memory much magnified – such ringing of bells, such public joy and sermons in memory of her, the picture of her tomb painted in many churches, more joy in memory of her coronation than for the coming in of King James.

▲ The historian Godfrey Goodman wrote this in a book published in 1839.

Source 5

Whereas Tudor governments got things done, Stuart politicians fumbled. The simple fact is: while Elizabeth lived, it worked.

▲ The historian John Guy compares Elizabeth's governments with that of her Stuart successors, *Tudor England*, 1988.

Source 6

▲ A portrait of Elizabeth by an unknown artist. the shadowy figures of 'Time' and 'Death' lurk behind the ageing Queen.

Read the sources on these pages and also look back at Chapter I.

1 Read Source 1. Does what you have learned about Elizabeth I support her own conclusion that she had reigned with her people's loves? Had she, also, been a 'careful and loving monarch'? Explain your answers in as much detail as you can.

2 Read Source 1 on page 14 and Source 2 on page 92.
   a What differences can you find between these two sources?
   b What reasons can you suggest for these differences?
   c Explain which of these two sources you think is more reliable in the judgements which the authors make about Elizabeth I.

3 Look again at Source 5 on page 14. Read Source 4 on this page. Use these sources, and your own knowledge, to explain why historians writing more than a century apart agree that Elizabeth I was more popular when she came to the throne than when she died.

4 Look at Source 6.
   a What point is the artist trying to make?
   b Compare Source 6 with the portrait of Elizabeth in Source 4 on page 13. Why do you think they are so different?

5 Look back at chapters 2 and 6. Why do you think that Elizabeth managed despite all challenges and rebellions to remain generally well-respected and obeyed until her death in 1603?

6 Why do people remember Elizabeth I? Use your answers to Questions 1-4 and any other evidence which you have found to explain your answer.

GLOSSARY

abdicate to give up being king or queen.

able-bodied poor poor people who were fit and well.

almshouses small houses specially built for the old or the sick by a well-off local person.

Assize Courts courts which travelled round the country to hear very serious cases sent up to them by the Justices of the Peace at the Quarter Sessions.

'auld alliance' friendship between France and Scotland which had existed for many centuries.

borough a town which had privileges granted by a monarch. The most important of these was that it could have a Member of Parliament.

bubonic plague a disease which was carried by rats and spread to humans by fleas. In 1348 the outbreak of the plague known as the 'Black Death' killed nearly half of the population of the country. Outbreaks continued, on a smaller scale, until the last great plague in 1665.

Casket Letters letters found in a silver casket in 1567. They were said to prove that Mary Queen of Scots had been involved in the murder of her second husband, Lord Darnley.

census an official count of the population.

'chain of being' the way in which God has created order on earth. It showed how all people and creatures were connected, in order, from God down to those in hell.

Churchwardens representatives of the parish who were responsible for looking after the church and the running of its services. In Elizabeth's reign they also had to collect poor relief.

colonies lands in newly discovered parts of the world that were claimed and then looked after by European countries - at this time mainly Portugal and Spain.

Common Law a collection of laws based on the decisions of the courts made over hundreds of years. This formed the basis of the English legal system. The rules made by the courts, which form the Common Law, are different from the laws made by parliament, which are called Statute Law.

consecration the central part of the Christian Holy Communion service when the bread and the wine are offered to God and become sacred.

couriers fast-travelling messengers who carried letters and parcels on horse-back.

Court of Common Pleas one of the courts of Common Law, based at Westminster. It decided disputes over e.g. land and debts.

Court of the King's Bench one of the courts of Common Law, based at Westminster. It was the most important criminal court in the land.

dissolution of the monasteries the closure of all the monasteries in England and Wales by Henry VIII between 1536 and 1540.

dynasty a family line of several generations, usually a royal or ruling family.

East India Company formed in 1600 to trade with the Spice Islands in the Indian Ocean.

enclosure movement during the late 18th and early 19th centuries Acts of Parliament were passed to turn thousands of acres of open fields, which were farmed together by villagers, into separate fields. These then made up farms owned by individual landowners.

excommunicated a person was banned by the Pope from attending Mass, receiving the sacraments, and mixing with other Catholics.

heretic someone who thinks and behaves in a way unacceptable to the Roman Catholic Church. Elizabeth was accused of being a heretic by Pope Pius V.

Holy Communion the church service when the priest gives the consecrated bread and wine to the people.

Holy Roman Empire an area roughly corresponding to Belgium, Holland, Germany, Austria and Hungary today (see map on page 57).

House of Commons the lower house of Parliament with elected members from the shires and the boroughs.

House of Correction these were set up in every county by the 1576 Poor Law Act. They were intended for the impotent poor who had refused to work.

House of Lords the upper house of Parliament, consisting of lords, bishops and judges.

impotent poor people like the sick and disabled, and old people and orphans, none of whom could look after themselves.

injunctions orders about changes to be made to church affairs, issued by the monarch.

Jesuits priests who were members of the Society of Jesus, the Catholic teaching order founded in 1534 by the Spanish priest Ignatius Loyola.

Justices of the Peace three or four important local men appointed by the Queen in each shire to keep 'the Queen's Peace'. They heard criminal cases brought before them and imprisoned those who were guilty. During Elizabeth's reign they also had to carry out the poor laws.

Levant Company a trading company started in 1581 to trade with the Turkish Empire.

Lord Lieutenant the royal representative in each shire, appointed by the monarch and usually a nobleman.

Mass the name given by the Roman Catholic Church to the service of Holy Communion.

missionary priests Catholic priests who were trained abroad and returned to England to try to convert English people back to Catholicism.

Oath of Supremacy part of the Act of Parliament of 1559 which set up the Church of England. All clergymen had to swear to accept Elizabeth as Supreme Governor of the Church of England. Later, all officials, lawyers and MPs had to take the oath.

pageants colourful local events which included processions and plays.

Papal Bull a written order from the Pope, which all members of the Roman Catholic Church had to obey.

paupers able-bodied poor who wanted to find work but could not. In Elizabeth's reign these people began to receive help from the parishes.

Pilgrimage of Grace a widespread northern rising which took place in 1536-37. There were many causes, but some of these were protests against Henry VIII's religious changes, including the dissolution of the monasteries.

poor-rate money collected in towns and parishes to help to support the disabled and impotent poor.

Pope the head of the Roman Catholic Church.

proclamations measures announced by the monarch which have the force of law. They deal with emergencies or make laws when Parliament is not in session.

Protestantism the name of the Christian movement which broke away from the Roman Catholic Church during the 16th century Reformation.

Puritans extreme Protestants who wanted to 'purify' the church, to set up simple services and ensure that people were helped to follow the teachings of the Bible.

Quarter Sessions courts held four times a year in each county by two or more Justices of the Peace. These courts dealt with serious crimes sent up to them by individual JPs in the shires.

'Queen's Peace' law and order in the name of the Queen.

recusants Roman Catholics who refused to attend Church of England Services and continued with their old religious beliefs and practices.

Reformation the 16th century movement which led to the setting up of Protestant Churches which rejected the teachings of the Catholic Church and the authority of the Pope.

Roman Catholic Church the name given to the Christian Church of Western Europe, led by the Pope. In the 16th century, the Reformation led to a splitting of the Western European Church into Catholic and Protestant churches.

Royal Assent the agreement which has to be given by the monarch to every bill passed by Parliament before it can become law.

sacraments the outward, visible signs of sacred gifts from God which help people to live a Godly life. These include Baptism, Confirmation, Holy Communion and Marriage.

Spanish Armada the fleet sent against England by Philip II of Spain in July 1558.

sturdy beggars fit and healthy beggars who did not want to work.

surplice a loose, white over-tunic with wide sleeves, worn by priests and ministers during church services.

vagabonds able-bodied, wandering beggars who roamed the countryside looking for food and shelter.

Wars of the Roses the series of battles which took place during the second half of the 15th century between the noble families of York (represented by a white rose) and Lancaster (represented by a red rose). Henry VII claimed to be a Lancastrian and so brought about the 'union of the roses' by marrying Elizabeth of York.

yeoman a quite well-off farmer, who might own his own farm or rent it, as a tenant farmer, from a richer landowner.

INDEX